Cultural Atlas for Young People

ANCIENT AMERICA

Marion Wood

Facts On File, Inc.

Managing Editor: Lionel Bender
Art Editor: Ben White
Designer: Malcolm Smythe
Text Editor: Alison Freegard
Assistant Editor: Madeleine Samuel
Project Editor: Graham Bateman
Cartographic Manager: Olive Pearson
Cartographic Editor: Zoë Goodwin
Design Consultant: John Ridgeway
Production: Clive Sparling

Advisory Editor of the series: Gillian Evans,
Fitzwilliam College, Cambridge
Advisory Editor for this volume: Warwick Bray,
Institute of Archaeology, London

Planned and produced by:
Andromeda Oxford Ltd.
11–13 The Vineyard
Abingdon
Oxfordshire OX14 3PX
England

Prepared by Lionheart Books

Media conversion and typesetting:
Peter MacDonald, Una Macnamara
and Vanessa Hersey

Library of Congress Cataloging-in-Publication
Data

Wood, Marion.
     Ancient America / Marion Wood.
     p. cm.--(Cultural Atlas for young
people)
     Includes bibliographical references.
     Summary: Maps and text offer
information on the cultures and histories of
native groups in both North and South
America.
     ISBN 0-8160-2210-0
     1. Indians--Antiquities--Juvenile
literature. 2. America--Antiquities--Juvenile
literature. [1. Indians--Antiquities. 2.
America--Antiquities.] I. Title. II. Series.
E61.W9   1990
970.01--dc20   90-2957
                                              CIP
                                              AC

Published in North America by
Facts On File, Inc.
11 Penn Plaza
New York, N.Y. 10001

Origination by J. Film Process,
Singapore

Printed in China
9 8 7 6 5 4

Artwork and Picture Credits
All maps drawn by Lovell Johns, Oxford.

Key: t = top, b = bottom, c = center, l = left, r = right etc.

Title page, 5: Werner Forman Archive, London. 6,7 Malcolm Smythe. 8 Smithsonian Institution, Washington. 10l Kevin Maddison. 10r Werner Forman Archive, London. 11 Fred Bruemmer, Montreal. 12l Equinox Picture Archive, Oxford. 12r Fotomas Index, London. 14 Simon Driver, Oxford. 14-15 Robert Harding Picture Library, London. 16l Susan Griggs Agency, London. 16r Walter Rawlings/Robert Harding Picture Library, London. 17 Zefa, London. 19tl Werner Forman Archive, London. 19tr Kevin Maddison. 19cl Dick Barnard, Milverton. 19bl Dirk Bakker, Detroit Institute of Arts. 21 Kevin Maddison. 22 t,b Fred Bruemmer, Montreal. 23 Kevin Maddison. 24l Dirk Bakker, Detroit Institute of Arts. 24r Museum of the American Indian, Heye Foundation. 26t Werner Forman Archive, London. 26b, 28-29 Kevin Maddison. 29t Dirk Bakker, Detroit Institute of Arts. 29cr Dick Barnard, Milverton. 29br Dirk Bakker, Detroit Institute of Arts. 30 Dick Barnard, Milverton. 31 Kevin Maddison. 32 Werner Forman Archive, London. 33t Royal Anthropological Institute of Great Britain and Ireland. 33b Kevin Maddison. 34, 34-35 Fotomas Index, London. 35t Equinox Picture Archive, Oxford. 37tl Lee Boltin, Croton-on-Hudson, New York. 37tr John Fuller, Cambridge. 37b Kevin Maddison. 38-39t Walter Rawlings/Robert Harding Picture Library, London. 38-39b Kevin Maddison. 40,40-41 Justin Kerr, New York. 41 Kevin Maddison. 42 David Muench, Santa Barbara. 43 Werner Forman Archive, London. 44 Walter Rawlings/Robert Harding Picture Library, London. 44-45 Chris Forsey. 45 Werner Forman Archive, London. 46tr Lee Boltin, Croton-on-Hudson, New York. 46b Joseph Mora. 47t Smithonian Institution, Washington. 47b Kevin Maddison. 48 Werner Forman Archive, London. 49l Dean Snow, Albany, New York. 49tr Werner Forman Archive, London. 49br Lee Boltin, Croton-on-Hudson, New York. 50 Equinox Picture Archive, Oxford/Museum of the American Indian, Heye Foundation. 50-51 Michael Coe, New Haven. 52 Walter Rawlings/Robert Harding Picture Library, London. 53b Tony Morrison, South American Pictures. 55t, c Michael Coe, New Haven. 55b Kevin Maddison. 56t Dumbarton Oaks, Washington. 56b William R. O'Boyle, New Haven. 58l Michael Coe, New Haven. 58r Roy C. Craven Jr, Gainesville, Florida. 59 Michael Coe, New Haven. 60 Lee Boltin, Croton-on-Hudson, New York. 61 Chris Forsey. 62t Nicholas Helmuth, New Haven. 62b,63 Simon Driver. 64t, 64b Marion and Tony Morrison, Woodbridge. 65l Werner Forman Archive, London. 65r Michael Coe, New Haven. 66 Marion and Tony Morrison, Woodbridge. 67 Lee Boltin, Croton-on-Hudson, New York. 68t Michael Coe, New Haven. 68b,69t Michael Holford, Loughton. 69b Justin Kerr, New York. 71t Werner Forman Archive, London. 71b Lee Boltin, Croton-on-Hudson, New York. 72-73 Kevin Maddison. 73 British Museum, London. 74t Warwick Bray, London. 74b Marion and Tony Morrison, Woodbridge. 76t Michael Coe, New Haven. 76b Kevin Maddison. 77tl,tr Lee Boltin, Croton-on-Hudson, New York. 77b Justin Kerr. 78 Lee Boltin, Croton-on-Hudson, New York. 79tl Marion and Tony Morrison, Woodbridge. 79tr Johan Reinhard, Lima. 79b Kevin Maddison. 80tl,tr Linden Museum, Stuttgart. 80b Warwick Bray, London. 81t, c,b Marion and Tony Morrison, Woodbridge. 83t Marion Morrison. 83bl Marion and Tony Morrison, Woodbridge. 83br Michael Coe, New Haven. 84t Marion and Tony Morrison, Woodbridge. 84b Tom Owen Edmunds, London. 84-85 W. Janoud/Zefa. 86 Elizabeth Benson, Washington. 87 Kevin Maddison. 88, 89tl Lee Boltin, Croton-on-Hudson, New York. 89tr Werner Forman Archive, London. 89bl Linden Museum, Stuttgart. 89br Robert Harding Picture Library, London. 90t Neil Stevenson. 90b Michael Coe, New Haven. 91t Robert Harding Picture Library, London. 91bl Robin Bath/ Robert Harding Picture Library, London. 91cr Justin Kerr, New York. 94 Kurt Goebel/Zefa.

CONTENTS

INTRODUCTION

This book is about ancient America. Although we often talk of Christopher Columbus "discovering" America in 1492, prehistoric hunters in search of food had crossed into northwest America from Asia thousands of years earlier. By the time Columbus arrived, there were millions of people living all over America. Columbus called these people Indians, because he thought that he had traveled round the world and had landed in the East Indies.

We cannot lump together the ancient Americans as we might the ancient Greeks or ancient Romans. There were (and are) many American Indian peoples, speaking separate languages and living in very different ways. In this book you will read about the most important of those that lived in the period from the end of the Ice Age to the beginning of European exploration and conquest in the late 15th century. Over these 12,000 years each group of ancient Americans developed skills and traditions best suited to their environment and its resources. Many were nomadic hunters and gatherers of wild plants. A number were farmers who lived in well-organized towns and villages. Some were skilled craftsmen, producing fine pottery or textiles or working in precious metals. Others built great cities and ruled vast empires.

How do we learn about these peoples of ancient America and their ways of life? Some of them, like the Maya and the Aztec, used picture-writing to record important events, and we can interpret this. But the majority had no form of writing at all. For the most part, therefore, we must depend on archaeological evidence, but this also varies greatly. Some ancient Americans are well represented by the remains of their stone buildings, carvings, textiles, pottery and metalwork. Others, like the nomadic hunters who lived in skin tents or brushwood shelters, have left little trace behind. Not surprisingly, we know more about the first group than we do about the second.

Ancient America begins with a short overview of the early history of the whole of the American continent. Then the book is divided into two main sections. The first, **The History of North America**, looks in detail at the people and places of the North American subcontinent. The second section, **The History of Latin America**, deals with Mesoamerica and South America, in particular with the great civilizations like those of the Aztec in Mexico and the Inca in Peru. You may find some of our terms confusing. "Latin America" means those areas where languages derived from Latin, such as Spanish and Portuguese, are now spoken – Mexico, Central America (from Guatemala to Panama) South America and some of the Caribbean Islands. "Mesoamerica" refers to those parts of Mexico and Central America that were civilized before the Spanish Conquest.

This book is an atlas. There are lots of maps to help you understand what was happening in different parts of America at different times. Many of the maps are accompanied by charts giving important dates or useful information. Our story is arranged in double-page spreads. Each spread is a complete story. So you can either read the book from beginning to end or just dip into it to learn about a specific topic. The Glossary on page 92 contains definitions of some of the terms used in the book. If you want to look up a particular place on a map, the Gazetteer on page 93 will tell you where to find it.

Abbreviations used in this book
AD = Anno Domini (the year of the Lord; of the Christian era).
BC = Before Christ. c. = circa (about). in = inch. ft = foot.
yd = yard. mi = mile.

▷ Pueblo Indian cliff dwellings at Mesa Verde in Colorado, North America, from about AD 1000.

4

TABLE OF DATES

	1500 BC	1200 BC	1000 BC	800 BC	500 BC	100 BC
NORTH AMERICA	Poverty Point built c.1500.	End of Archaic period c.1200-1000.	Dorset people begin to spread over eastern Arctic c.1000.	Adena people in Ohio valley c.700.	Large villages such as Ipiutak built in Alaska c.500. Woodlands farmers move westwards into Plains c.250.	Hopewell people i valley c.100. Southwestern farm (Hohokam, Mog Anasazi) c.100.
	Stone spearhead from Folsom, New Mexico c.9000 BC.	Clay figurine from Poverty Point c.1500 BC.			Ivory snow goggles and boss from Ipiutak, Alaska c.500 BC-AD 500.	
MESOAMERICA	Development of Olmec civilization. San Lorenzo founded c.1500.		Olmec site of La Venta founded c.900.		Decline of Olmec civilization c.400. Development of early Maya civilization c.300.	
	Carving of trophy head from Cerro Sechin, Peru c.1300 BC.		Bowl from Tlapacoya, Valley of Mexico c.1200-900 BC.		Olmec head, La Venta c.900-400 BC.	
SOUTH AMERICA	Oldest known metalwork c.1500.	Development of Chavín civilization c.1200.	Chavín de Huantar founded c.850.	Paracas tombs c.700-200.	Nazca people on south coast of Peru c.370 BC-AD 450. Decline of Chavín de Huantar c.200.	Arawak Indians arrive in Antilles c.100.

Row 1 (top text band):

AD 500	AD 800	AD 1000	AD 1200	AD 1500
Thule people appear in Alaska c.500. Cahokia founded c.600.	Mississippian towns built c.800. Farming villages in eastern Plains. Chaco Canyon towns built c.900-1100.	Northern Iroquoians settle around Great Lakes c.1000. Thule people begin to spread over eastern Arctic c.1000. Norse settlement in Newfoundland c.1000. Cliff dwellings at Mesa Verde and Canyon de Chelly c.1100.	Drought in Southwest 1276-1299. Cliff dwellings abandoned c.1300. Decline of Cahokia c.1450.	Cartier explores St Lawrence valley 1535-1536. De Soto explores Southeast 1539-1542. Coronado explores Southwest and southern Plains 1540-1542.

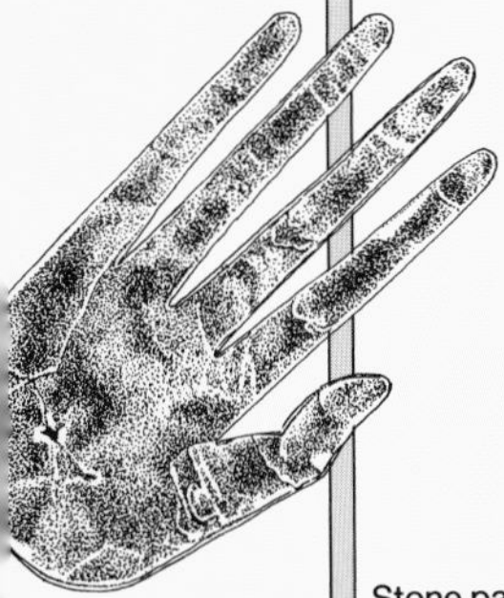

Illustration captions (band 2):

...hand, Hopewell ...ture, 100 BC-AD 600.

Stone paint palette from Snaketown c.AD 100-500.

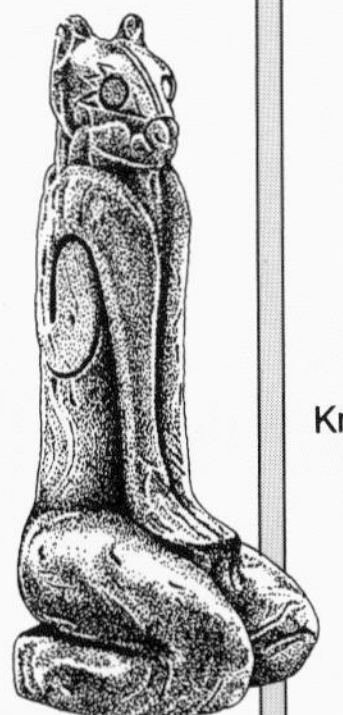

Kneeling cat figure from Key Marco, Florida c.AD 800-1500.

Cliff Palace, Mesa Verde c.AD 1100.

Row 3 (middle text band):

AD 1	AD 500	AD 800	AD 1000	AD 1200	AD 1500
Teotihuacan founded c.150. Development of Classic Maya civilization c. 300.	Reign of Pacal at Palenque 618-653.	Teotihuacan destroyed c. 750. Collapse of lowland Maya civilization c.900. Toltec city of Tula founded c.950.	Tula destroyed 1168.	Decline of Maya civilization in Yucatan c.1200. Aztec city of Tenochtitlan founded c.1345. Aztecs control Valley of Mexico 1428.	Aztec empire reaches greatest extent 1502. Cortes invades Mexico 1519. Spaniards conquer Mexico and destroy Aztec empire 1519-1521.

Illustration captions (band 4):

...house model, ...uador c.500 BC- ...500.

Moche pot c.AD 100-500.

Lord Chac Zutz from Palenque AD 730.

Inca silver statuette c.AD 1400-1520.

Row 5 (bottom text band):

AD 1	AD 500	AD 800	AD 1000	AD 1200	AD 1500
...he people on north ...ast of Peru c.1-600.	Development of Tiahuanaco and Huari c.500.	Huari abandoned c.800.	Decline of Tiahuanaco c.1000.	Carib Indians arrive in Antilles c.1200. Inca city of Cuzco founded 1200. Columbus lands in Bahamas 1492.	Spaniards conquer Peru and destroy Inca empire 1532.

7

THE LAND AND PEOPLE

The entire length of America measures about 9,000 mi from the Arctic Ocean to the tip of South America. Over this vast distance there are many changes of climate and landscape. There are icy wastes, fertile river valleys, tropical forests, grasslands, and deserts.

The American Indians, who arrived long before European explorers, lived in different ways according to their environment.

Hunters and farmers

Some of the early Indian peoples, like the Shoshone who lived in the deserts west of the Rocky Mountains, were nomadic hunters and gatherers, wandering in search of the animals and plants that they needed for food. They carried their few belongings on their backs and camped in simple brushwood shelters.

Others, like the Aztecs, who settled in the fertile Valley of Mexico, were farmers, living in permanent villages near their fields. They were also fierce warriors who fought neighboring peoples and seized their lands. In time they founded a great empire which controlled a large part of Central America for a hundred years.

▷ The Rocky Mountains and the Andes are part of the same mountain chain that runs along the western side of the North and South American continents like a giant backbone. The mountains on the eastern side are less dramatic, with the Appalachian Mountains in the north and the Brazilian Highlands in the south. In between, the land is mainly low-lying with broad valleys drained by great rivers like the Mississippi, the Amazon, and the Orinoco.

◁ In the forests of Ecuador the waters of a mountain stream rush down to join the distant Amazon, eventually reaching the Atlantic Ocean 4,000 mi away. The forest Indians were both hunters and farmers. By cutting down trees and burning the undergrowth, they made clearings where they could plant crops and build their houses. When the land was exhausted, or used up, they moved on to clear another part of the forest.

◁ In this early 20th-century photo, an Inuit (Eskimo) craftsman uses old skills to make a cribbage score board for sale to tourists. The Inuits, who were hunters, invented many ingenious tools to help them overcome their harsh environment, such as the bow drill, which was used to make holes in tough materials. Here, the string of the bow is twisted around the drill shaft which this craftsman holds in his mouth. As he moves the bow back and forth the shaft rotates and its metal point drills into the walrus tusk.

ARCTIC OCEAN

A | B | C | D | E | F

GREENLAND
(Denmark)

7

Baffin
Island

ICELAND

ALASKA
Yukon
Mt McKinley
△ 6194
ALASKA RANGE

Mackenzie

MACKENZIE MTS

Gt Bear Lake

Gt Slave Lake

Hudson
Bay

Labrador

COAST MTS

ROCKY MOUNTAINS

Great

CANADA

L Athabasca

L Winnipeg

Newfoundland

6

Cascade Range

Plains

L Superior

Ottawa
St Lawrence

Sierra Nevada

Great
Basin

Missouri

L Michigan

L Huron

UNITED STATES
OF AMERICA

Ohio

L Ontario
L Erie

APPALACHIAN MTS

Washington

ATLANTIC OCEAN

5

Rio Grande

Sierra Madre Occidental

MEXICO

Sierra Madre Oriental

Gulf of Mexico

BAHAMAS

Havana
CUBA

Mexico City
Valley of
Mexico

BELIZE
Belmopan

JAMAICA

DOMINICAN REPUBLIC
HAITI
Port-au-
Prince
Santo Domingo

Puerto
Rico
(USA)

Lesser
Antilles

Guatemala City
GUATEMALA
HONDURAS
Tegucigalpa
San Salvador
NICARAGUA
EL SALVADOR
Managua
COSTA RICA
San José
Panamá
PANAMA

Caribbean Sea

Caracas

Orinoco

TRINIDAD
AND TOBAGO

4

PACIFIC OCEAN

Bogotá

VENEZUELA

Georgetown

GUYANA

Paramaribo

SURINAM

Cayenne
FRENCH
GUIANA

COLOMBIA

GUIANA HIGHLANDS

Galapagos Is

Quito

Japurá

ECUADOR

Ucayali

Selvas

Madeira

Amazon

Araguaia

BRAZIL

BRAZILIAN HIGHLANDS

3

Meters
4000
1000
200
0
2000 Sea depth

─ · ─ International boundary

■ Capital city

△6550 Mountain peak (meters)

Equatorial scale 1 : 54 000 000

PERU

ANDES

Lima

L Titicaca

Ancohuma
△6550
La Paz

Paraguay

Brasília

BOLIVIA

PARAGUAY

Asunción

Paraná

2

ANDES

Aconcagua
△6960

URUGUAY

Montevideo

Santiago

Buenos Aires

CHILE

ARGENTINA

Falkland Is
(UK)

1

Cape Horn

9

THE FIRST AMERICANS

The first people to reach America came on foot from Asia during the last Ice Age more than 25,000 years ago. These two continents were not then separated by sea as they are now, but were linked by a bridge of land, about 930 mi wide, known as Beringia. Grazing herds of Ice Age animals, like mammoth, mastodon, caribou, and bison, wandered over the grassy surface of the land bridge. In pursuit of them came small bands of nomadic hunters. These were the ancestors of the American Indians.

Over the land bridge

Unlike later Europeans, these early hunters were not explorers or conquerers seeking a new world. They were simply following the game herds that they needed for food. It was not a mass invasion. They came in small family groups, a few people at a time. They pitched their camps of skin tents for only as long as they needed to, moving on as the herds moved. In this way, they gradually crossed over the land bridge into what is now Alaska.

Over thousands of years their descendants, gradually increasing in number, spread southwards into the heart of the continent. By 18,000 BC they had arrived in Mexico, and around 12,000 years ago they had reached the very southernmost tip of South America.

The end of the Ice Age

Around 10,000 years ago the Ice Age ended. As the ice melted, sea levels rose. The land bridge between Asia and America was flooded and the Bering Strait came into being. The campsites of the very first Americans disappeared under the sea forever. Latecomers to America, like the Inuit (Eskimos) (see pages 20-23), had to cross over from Asia by boat.

Over the following centuries changes in climate affected the landscape and wildlife throughout the northern hemisphere. In many areas, forests replaced grasslands, for example, and huge grazing animals like the mammoth died out as their food supply dwindled.

▽ Stone spearheads like this were used by the first Americans to hunt large animals. Some have been found among the bones of animals killed by people more than 10,000 years ago, about the time the last Ice Age ended.

◁ The first people to inhabit the cold plains of Ice Age America were small bands of nomadic hunters. The animals they hunted with their stone-tipped spears provided food for their families, as well as skins for tents and for warm clothing.

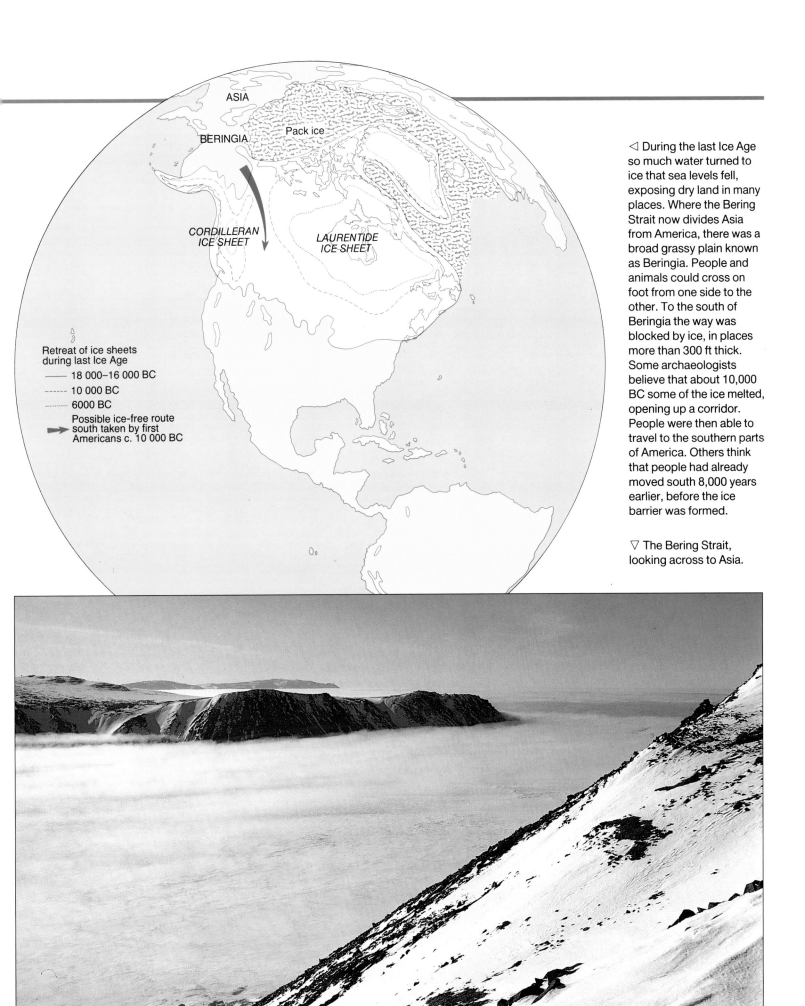

ASIA

BERINGIA

Pack ice

CORDILLERAN
ICE SHEET

LAURENTIDE
ICE SHEET

Retreat of ice sheets
during last Ice Age
—— 18 000–16 000 BC
----- 10 000 BC
········ 6000 BC
➤ Possible ice-free route
south taken by first
Americans c. 10 000 BC

◁ During the last Ice Age so much water turned to ice that sea levels fell, exposing dry land in many places. Where the Bering Strait now divides Asia from America, there was a broad grassy plain known as Beringia. People and animals could cross on foot from one side to the other. To the south of Beringia the way was blocked by ice, in places more than 300 ft thick. Some archaeologists believe that about 10,000 BC some of the ice melted, opening up a corridor. People were then able to travel to the southern parts of America. Others think that people had already moved south 8,000 years earlier, before the ice barrier was formed.

▽ The Bering Strait, looking across to Asia.

EARLY EXPLORATION AND CONQUEST

Vikings from Norse settlements in Greenland explored the Labrador and Newfoundland coasts about AD 1000. They settled at L'Anse aux Meadows, but then returned to Greenland.

Columbus and the "conquistadores"
In 1492 Christopher Columbus landed in the Bahamas. He claimed these islands for his master the King of Spain. Mistakenly believing that he had found a new route to India, he called the native Americans "Indians." Columbus's voyages opened the way for European exploration and conquest.

All the Caribbean islands were soon under Spanish rule. From their base in Hispaniola, the *conquistadores* launched a series of invasions of the mainland. In 1519-21 Hernan Cortes conquered Mexico and destroyed the Aztec empire. In 1533 the Inca empire in Peru fell to Spanish forces led by Francisco Pizarro.

Several Spanish expeditions explored the southern parts of North America, hoping to find rich cities like those in Mexico and Peru.

Hernando de Soto, who had served under Pizarro in Peru, landed in Florida in 1539. He spent many months exploring the southeast, attacking and looting Indian villages. In 1541 he reached the Mississippi, but died in 1542.

In 1540-42 Francisco de Coronado and his men explored the southwest and the southern plains as far as Kansas. They captured several Indian villages but did not find the treasure they had hoped for. They returned to Mexico, disappointed and empty-handed.

▷ Many early explorers, like Ferdinand Magellan from Portugal and Francis Drake from England, sailed along the coasts and did not venture far inland. When explorers began to invade Indian lands, fighting broke out and hundred of Indians were killed. Many others died of European diseases against which they had no resistance. As a result, the Indian population fell dramatically during the 16th century. In Latin America many people are of mixed Indian and European descent. They are known as *mestizos*.

Jacques Cartier claimed land along the St. Lawrence river for France in the 1530s, but the European settlement of North America did not get under way until the next century.

◁ An Eastern Woodlands hunter painted by a 16th-century English explorer. He hunted chiefly buffalo and deer and wears a buffalo skin breechcloth. His face and body are painted. A wristguard protects his arm from the bowstring. His quiver is slung over his shoulder.

▽ Columbus's arrival in Hispaniola (which he called La Isla Espanõla) imagined by a 16th-century artist who never visited the Americas. He shows the Indians bringing gifts – of European jewelry and metalwork! In fact, they gave Columbus cotton thread, spears, and parrots.

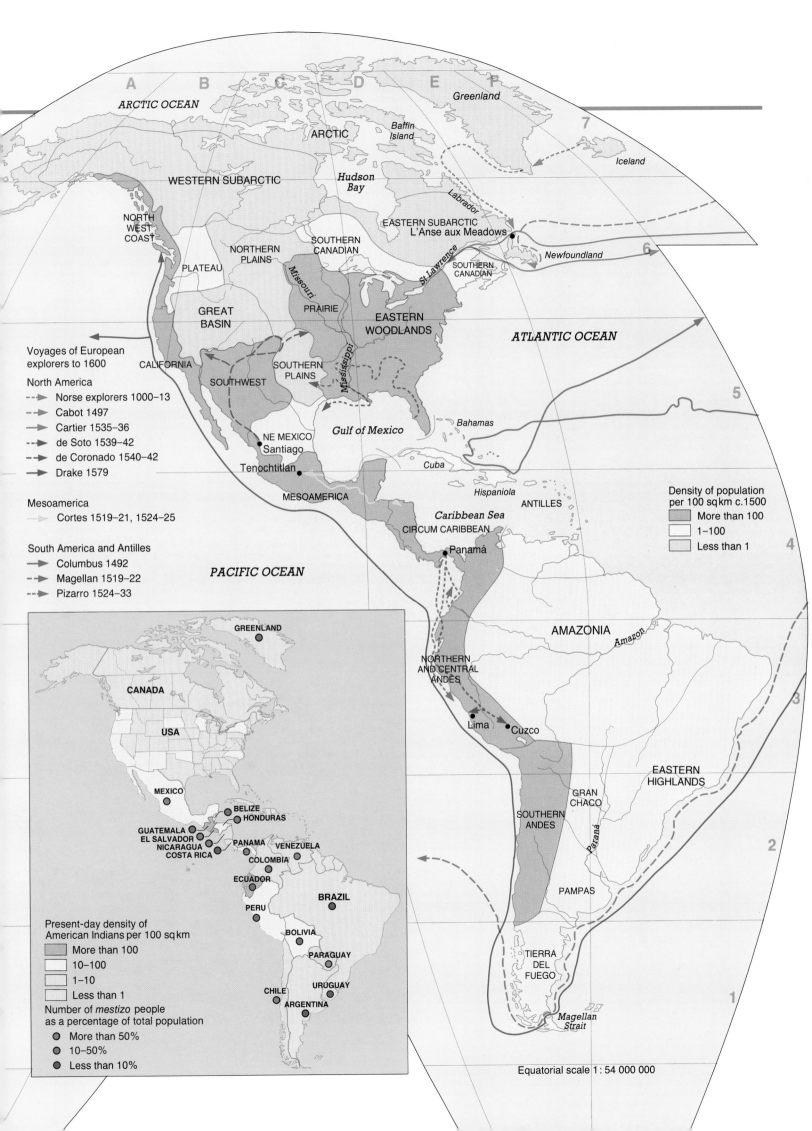

ARCTIC OCEAN

A B C D E F

7

Greenland

Baffin
Island

ARCTIC

Iceland

WESTERN SUBARCTIC

Hudson
Bay

Labrador

NORTH
WEST
COAST

EASTERN SUBARCTIC
L'Anse aux Meadows

6

PLATEAU

NORTHERN
PLAINS

SOUTHERN
CANADIAN

St Lawrence

SOUTHERN
CANADIAN

Newfoundland

Missouri

GREAT
BASIN

PRAIRIE

EASTERN
WOODLANDS

ATLANTIC OCEAN

Voyages of European
explorers to 1600

CALIFORNIA

SOUTHERN
PLAINS

Mississippi

5

North America

SOUTHWEST

→ Norse explorers 1000–13

→ Cabot 1497

→ Cartier 1535–36

→ de Soto 1539–42

→ de Coronado 1540–42

→ Drake 1579

Bahamas

NE MEXICO
Santiago

Gulf of Mexico

Cuba

Tenochtitlan

Hispaniola

ANTILLES

MESOAMERICA

Mesoamerica

→ Cortes 1519–21, 1524–25

Caribbean Sea

CIRCUM CARIBBEAN

Density of population
per 100 sq km c.1500

More than 100

1–100

Less than 1

4

South America and Antilles

→ Columbus 1492

→ Magellan 1519–22

→ Pizarro 1524–33

PACIFIC OCEAN

Panamá

AMAZONIA

Amazon

NORTHERN
AND CENTRAL
ANDES

Lima

Cuzco

3

EASTERN
HIGHLANDS

GREENLAND

GRAN
CHACO

Paraná

CANADA

USA

SOUTHERN
ANDES

2

MEXICO

PAMPAS

BELIZE
HONDURAS

GUATEMALA
EL SALVADOR
NICARAGUA
COSTA RICA

PANAMA
VENEZUELA

COLOMBIA

TIERRA
DEL
FUEGO

ECUADOR

BRAZIL

1

PERU

Present-day density of
American Indians per 100 sq km

BOLIVIA

Magellan
Strait

More than 100

PARAGUAY

10–100

URUGUAY

1–10

CHILE

Less than 1

ARGENTINA

Number of *mestizo* people
as a percentage of total population

● More than 50%

● 10–50%

● Less than 10%

Equatorial scale 1 : 54 000 000

PART ONE

THE HISTORY OF NORTH AMERICA

△ Feathered man, from a Southern Cult engraved shell dating from about AD 1100. The design reflects the Hopewell people's customs and beliefs but also has Mexican influences.

▷ Mt. McKinley, now known as often by its Indian name "Denali," rises 20,440 ft above central Alaska. This part of the Arctic was the homeland of the Athapascan Indians for thousands of years.

NORTH AMERICA : CLIMATE AND VEGETATION

Although the far north of the continent is cold throughout the year, most of North America has a temperate climate. There are cold winters, warm or hot summers, and pleasant spring and fall seasons. The rainfall varies. Most rain falls over the mountain ranges and along the coasts. Over the great central plain the climate is drier and in some areas, like the southwest, the land is semidesert or desert.

Coasts and forests

The Arctic landscape changes from ice and snow in the far north to the cold treeless plain known as the tundra, inhabited by the Inuit. Farther south, and stretching along the north Pacific coast, lie dense forests of pine, spruce, and cedar. On the other side of the country, from the Great Lakes south to the Gulf of Mexico, the land is also wooded, with some evergreens like spruce and fir. But broadleaved deciduous trees like birch and oak are more common. The groups of people who made up the Eastern Woodlands culture dwelt here (see pages 18-19 and 24-25).

Grasslands

Between the Rocky Mountains and the Mississippi river lies the area known as the Great Plains. The western or High Plains were dry and windswept with short coarse grass. But on the eastern prairies, the grass was thick and tall, growing nearly 7 ft high. Great buffalo herds, up to several million strong, once grazed here. By the end of the 19th century, due to overhunting by white hunters, buffalo were almost extinct. Today much of the land is cultivated and wheat and maize are grown over vast areas.

Southwestern deserts

Southwest of the Plains the land rises to form a high sandstone plateau cut by deep canyons. Rainfall is low here, but Indian farmers were able to grow maize and other crops by digging irrigation channels to water their fields.

West of the Rocky Mountains lies the Great Basin, the most barren area of North America. Today modern irrigation has made farming here possible, but in prehistoric times it was too dry for Indian methods of agriculture.

◁ The rugged coast of southeastern Alaska near the town of Juneau. During the last Ice Age this area was covered with great sheets of ice. Remnants of these ice sheets still exist as glaciers in some of the mountain valleys.

▽ Canyon de Chelly, 120 mi east of the Grand Canyon in Arizona. This landscape was sculpted by rivers when the climate was much wetter. Windblown sand has eroded the softer rock into strange shapes.

▷ The different types of natural environment found in North America have evolved over the past 10,000 years (after the last Ice Age ended). Changes in climate at various times have affected both plant and animal life.

As deserts appeared or as forests replaced grassland, some kinds of animals moved to other areas in search of new sources of food. Others died out altogether.

In turn, such changes affected the way people lived. Some people turned to hunting other animals and moved to new areas in pursuit of them. Others began to gather more wild plants and vegetables and in time became farmers.

Sometimes prehistoric Indians tried to alter the landscape themselves in order to improve their way of life. Hunters set fire to areas of forest to provide better grazing for the deer they hunted. Woodland farmers used fire to clear land for cultivation. In dry areas some dug irrigation channels to grow crops.

ARCTIC OCEAN

Bering Strait

Greenland

Iceland

Yukon

Mackenzie

Great Bear Lake

Great Slave Lake

Hudson Bay

PACIFIC OCEAN

Fraser

ROCKY MOUNTAINS

Great Plains

L Winnipeg

L Superior

L Huron

St Lawrence

Missouri

L Michigan

L Ontario

L Erie

Great Basin

Eastern Woodlands

Ohio

APPALACHIAN MTS

ATLANTIC OCEAN

Arkansas

Colorado

Mississippi

Rio Grande

Sierra Madre Occidental

Sierra Madre Oriental

Gulf of Mexico

☐ Tundra and ice
▨ Coniferous forest
▨ Mixed forest
▨ Tropical rainforest
☐ Grassland
☐ Semi-desert and scrub
☐ Desert

Scale 1 : 40 000 000
0   800km

0   600 miles

▷ The Yellowstone river near its source in the foothills of the Rocky Mountains. From here it flows through the northern Plains to join the Missouri river. Huge herds of buffalo once grazed in this area.

NORTH AMERICA AFTER THE ICE

By 8000 BC most of the big game animals like the horse, mammoth, and mastodon had died out. People turned to hunting a wider range of smaller animals. Since they no longer needed to follow the big game herds, their way of life became less nomadic. They began to restrict their wanderings to particular areas and to make the most of the various sources of food found there at different times of the year. They began to collect more wild plants for food, although they did not yet grow their own crops. This period is known as the Archaic.

Hunting and fishing

The most important animals for Archaic hunters were deer and caribou. They provided large amounts of meat and their skins could be turned into clothing and other useful items. But smaller game was also hunted, like rabbits, otters, beavers, raccoons, and several kinds of birds. In addition, the sea, lakes, and rivers supplied a whole variety of fish and shellfish.

As people varied their activities, they began to use more specialized weapons and tools. Stone-tipped spears were still the hunter's favorite weapon. Sometimes he used a spear thrower, which helped him to hurl his spear

▽ After the Ice Age, the climate and landscape became similar to those of today. People began to follow new ways of life. Some remained nomadic, constantly on the move in search of food. But in areas where there were plenty of animals and plants to eat, many people chose to remain in one place at least for part of the year. This map shows some of the places where they settled.

Life in the Archaic Period 8000-1000 BC

Subarctic Hunting, fishing and gathering people, small campsites.
Eastern Woodlands Hunting and gathering people, living in winter villages and traveling to summer campsites.
Plains Nomadic buffalo hunters, small campsites.
Northwest coast Hunting and fishing people, winter villages, and summer campsites.
Southwestern deserts Hunting and gathering, fishing along coast, cave shelters, and campsites.

◁ ▷ Danger Cave lies on the edge of the Great Salt Lake Desert in Utah. Bands of hunters and gatherers camped here from about 9000 BC and left many of their belongings behind. Even items that normally perish, like food, clothing, and baskets (*right*), have survived in the dry desert climate. In fact, so much survived here that by about AD 1, the cave was blocked by a heap of rubbish 14ft high.

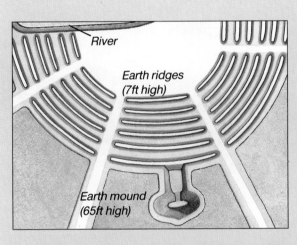

Earth ridges
(7ft high)

River

Earth mound
(65ft high)

Poverty Point

Poverty Point

At Poverty Point in Louisiana a large village grew up about 1500 BC. Huts were built along the top of six huge manmade ridges of earth, set one within the other (*above left*). The outermost ridge is about 4,300 ft across. The village people were hunters and fishermen.

Thousands of roughly shaped balls of clay have been found at Poverty Point. The villagers used these to cook their food. They first heated them in a fire and then dropped them into their cooking water to bring it to the required temperature. Some of the clay balls still bear finger marks of their makers. A few small clay figures (*left*) have also been found.

with more force than if he simply threw it by hand (see page 21). He also made nets, traps, and snares to catch small mammals, birds, and fish.

Using plants

People collected many kinds of fruit, seeds, and nuts according to the season. During this period they learned to prepare and cook food in new ways. Heavy grinding stones were used to crush or grind seeds and nuts into coarse flour, perhaps for making bread or porridge.

They also used grass and reeds for weaving baskets, bags and mats. They learned how to make their baskets waterproof by coating them with clay and how to boil water in them by dropping in heated stones or balls of clay. This method of cooking, known as "stone boiling," continued to be used in parts of North America right up until a hundred years ago.

Following the seasons

People moved according to the season, often following a set pattern. They had special places where they returned year after year.

In the Eastern Woodlands (see map) people lived in permanent base camps or villages during the winter and returned there after long hunting trips in summer.

People who lived in the southwestern deserts moved from one cave shelter to another during the course of a year. Often they left heavy tools and food supplies at each spot so that they did not have to carry too much with them as they traveled.

THE ARCTIC

The ancestors of today's Eskimos (see page 22) were the last native people to move into North America from Asia about 4000 BC. From Alaska they spread eastwards along the central Arctic coast, reaching Greenland around 2500 BC. Most modern Eskimos, now called the Inuit, are probably distant descendants of them.

The early Inuit were all nomadic hunters and fishermen. Some of their campsites have revealed small, finely worked tools and weapons and bones of the animals they hunted.

The eastern Arctic
The Dorset people, who take their name from Cape Dorset on Baffin Island, spread over much of Canada and Greenland from about 1000 BC. They were hunters of seal, walrus, and caribou. In summer they went on long hunting trips, living in skin tents. Although they had invented sledges, they had no dogs. They had to haul their equipment themselves. During the winter months they lived in villages. Their houses, partly underground for warmth, had walls of turf covered with skins. Inside each house there was an open hearth or fireplace in the middle of the floor and, around the walls, were benches for people to sit or sleep on.

The western Arctic and Thule expansion
From about 500 BC large villages were built along the Alaskan coast. Ipiutak on Point Hope perhaps had 700 houses. Many beautiful walrus bone and ivory carvings have been found in the burial ground at Ipiutak. For hunting seal and walrus, the Alaskan (Okvik) people used kayaks, light canoes made by stretching skins over a wooden framework. They also hunted whales, using larger open boats called umiaks, and used dogs to pull their sledges.

Thule, the name the Romans gave to the far north, is also the name given to late prehistoric Arctic peoples. The Thule people of Alaska were ingenious, rather warlike hunters who invented new types of bow and harpoon.

Around 1000 AD the Thule people began to move eastwards, perhaps seizing territory by force and conquering the inhabitants. Inuit legends tell of an earlier race of giants, the Tunit, who were driven away after fierce battles with Inuit ancestors. These tales may refer to encounters of the Dorset and Thule peoples.

▽ Most Inuit have always lived along the coasts of the tundra region, the treeless land beyond the northern limits of forest. The animals they hunted supplied them with all their needs. Over thousands of years they perfected a way of life ideally suited to the harsh Arctic environment.

Settlement in the Arctic 4000 BC to AD 1500

c. 4000-3000 BC The first Eskimos begin to move into America from Asia.
c. 2000 BC Eskimos reach the northern tip of Greenland.
c. 1000 BC to AD 1000 The Dorset people spread over the eastern Arctic.
c. 500 BC to AD 500 Large villages like Ipiutak are built along the coast of western Alaska.
c. 100 BC to AD 100 Okvik people settle in northern Alaska.
c. 500-1000 The Thule people appear in Alaska and spread all across the northern Arctic to Greenland.
c. 985 Norse settlers arrive in Greenland.
c. AD 1000-1500 The Thule people spread across the Arctic from Alaska to Greenland.
c. 1400 Norse settlements in Greenland are abandoned.

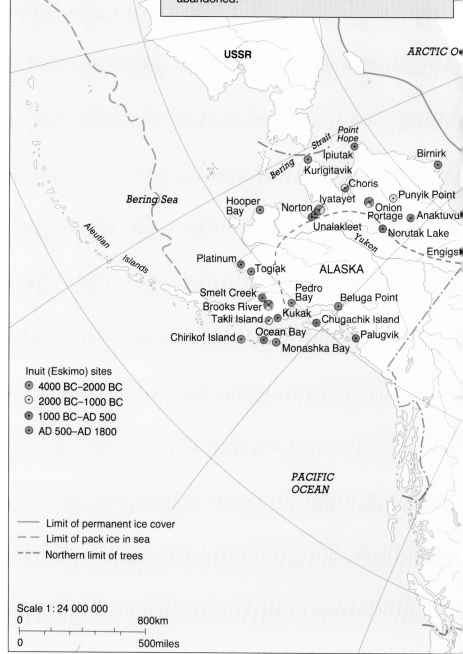

Inuit (Eskimo) sites
- 4000 BC–2000 BC
- 2000 BC–1000 BC
- 1000 BC–AD 500
- AD 500–AD 1800

— Limit of permanent ice cover
- - - Limit of pack ice in sea
– – – Northern limit of trees

Scale 1 : 24 000 000
0   800km
0   500miles

Inuit hunting tools
The Inuit used several kinds of harpoons and spears. A walrus harpoon had to be very strong to pierce the animal's thick hide. Spears for hunting seals and birds were smaller and lighter. Hunters used wooden spear throwers (*right*) to increase the spear's power. Each one was specially made for the hunter using it – its length equalled the distance between his forefinger and his elbow – and in effect gave him an extra arm joint.

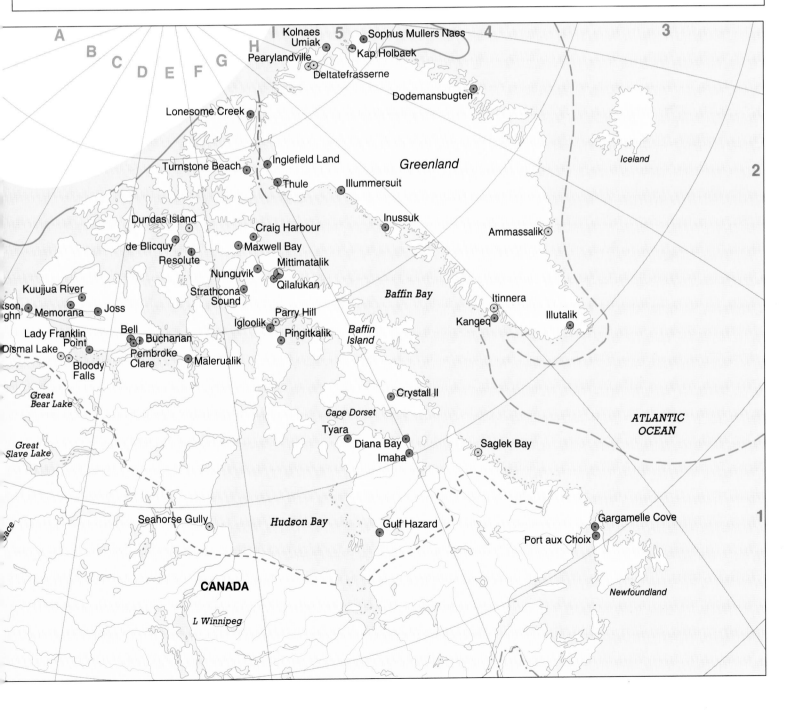

A B C D E F G H I 5 4 3 2 1

Kolnaes
Umiak
Sophus Mullers Naes
Kap Holbaek
Pearlandville
Deltatefrasserne
Dodemansbugten
Lonesome Creek
Inglefield Land
Greenland
Iceland
Turnstone Beach
Thule
Illummersuit
Dundas Island
Craig Harbour
Inussuk
Ammassalik
de Blicquy
Maxwell Bay
Resolute
Mittimatalik
Nunguvik
Qilalukan
Strathcona Sound
Baffin Bay
Itinnera
Kuujjua River
Parry Hill
Kangeq
Illutalik
son, ghn
Memorana
Joss
Igloolik
Pingitkalik
Baffin Island
Lady Franklin Point
Bell
Buchanan
Dismal Lake
Pembroke Clare
Maleruralik
Bloody Falls
Great Bear Lake
Crystall II
ATLANTIC OCEAN
Cape Dorset
Great Slave Lake
Tyara
Diana Bay
Imaha
Saglek Bay
Seahorse Gully
Hudson Bay
Gulf Hazard
Gargamelle Cove
Port aux Choix
CANADA
Newfoundland
L Winnipeg
ace

INUIT LIFE

Until the beginning of the 20th century, the Inuit (Eskimos) lived much as they had done for a thousand years. They depended for all their needs on success in hunting. Their whole way of life was geared to the seasonal movements of animals like seal and caribou.

In winter, seals were harpooned at their breathing holes in the ice. Great patience was needed. A hunter might have to stand motionless for hours, his harpoon at the ready, waiting for a seal to come up for air. In spring and summer the seals came out of the water to sun themselves on the ice. Hunters, making seal-like movements and noises, could crawl close up to them before throwing their harpoons.

Late summer was the main caribou hunting season. By then the animals were well fed, providing a supply of meat to store for the long winter months. Groups of hunters came together at camps near the caribou grazing grounds. They would all ambush the slow-moving herds with bows and arrows.

Protection from extreme cold

Warm clothing was just as important as food for survival. Sealskin was generally used for summer clothing, but in winter caribou skin was preferred. It was very warm, yet light to wear. Other skins used included those of musk oxen, polar bears, and birds. Women skinned the animals and cleaned the hides. They made all their family's clothing, stitching the skins with bone needles and gut thread. Both men and women wore hooded tunics and trousers over long boots. Women's tunics often had a very large hood for carrying a baby inside.

Inuit life today

With the growth of oil and mining industries in recent years, changes are taking place in the Arctic. Many Inuit now work in these industries. They live in modern houses and wear store-bought clothes. When they go hunting, they are more likely to use guns than harpoons or bows and arrows.

At the same time the Inuit are proud of their traditional ways. Many no longer wish to be called "Eskimo," the name first given to them by neighboring Indians. They prefer to be known by the name they call themselves, "Inuit," meaning simply "the people."

▷ An Inuit fisherman bobs a lure at the edge of the ice to attract fish. He will catch them using his leister, a special type of fishing spear like the one in the foreground. The fish is impaled on the central spike and the side pieces stop it from wriggling free.

▽ Inuit in the Baffin Bay area still use dog teams for pulling sledges and other heavy loads. Here hunters are using their dogs to haul the carcasses of walruses they have just killed. A dog team may consist of as many as 14 animals harnessed in a "fan" formation. In most other areas motor sledges have replaced dog teams.

▷ ▽ In summer some Inuit still live in tents of seal or caribou skin draped over frameworks of wood or bone and weighted down with stones. When winter comes, they build houses of stones covered with turf. Although "igloo" is an Inuit word for any kind of house, it has come to mean one made of snow.

The Inuit build these snow houses as temporary shelters when traveling in winter. They cut blocks of hard-packed snow and arrange them in a circle. More blocks are laid on top, rising in a spiral to form a dome. The last block at the top is fitted by a man working from inside. He then cuts his way out and forms the entrance tunnel.

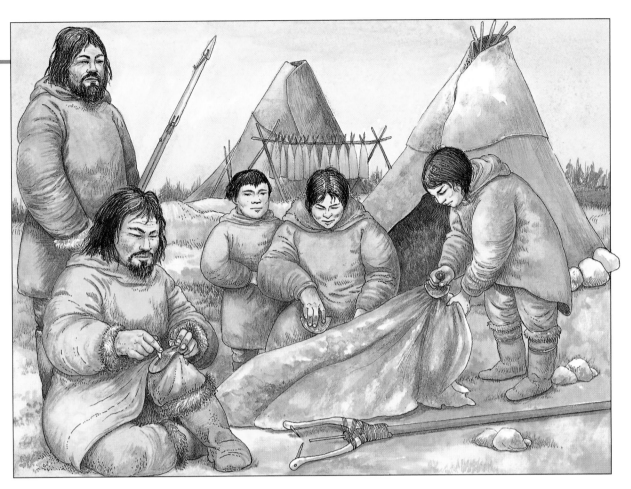

23

THE BURIAL MOUND BUILDERS

By about 1000 BC well-organized farming communities were being established in the Eastern Woodlands. As well as gathering wild plants for food, these people also grew crops in fields near their villages. The Adena lived in the Ohio Valley from about 700 BC. They hunted and fished, and grew a number of food crops, such as squash, gourds, and sunflowers (for both seeds and roots). The Hopewell people who came after them around 100 BC grew maize as well. Their culture reached along the Mississippi and its tributaries.

Earthworks and burial mounds
The Adena and Hopewell farmers enjoyed a settled and prosperous way of life. The huge earthworks that they built can still be seen today. Those built by the Hopewell people are especially large and elaborate. Some are enclosures, perhaps built for holding important

▷ (map) The Adena and Hopewell peoples set up trading links with distant people and places in order to obtain the raw materials that they needed, such as mica, copper, and shells. Merchants traveled to these outlying places to exchange the finished goods for such raw materials. The people who had acquired these goods began to make copies of them and to follow the customs of their makers. This was how the way of life of the Adena and Hopewell peoples spread far beyond the Ohio Valley.

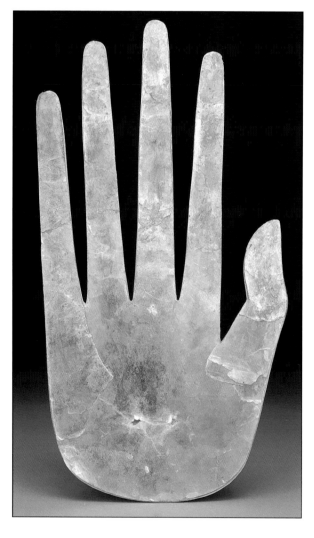

◁ This hand is cut from mica, a type of mineral found in rocks which then is split into thin transparent sheets. It may have been a badge of office or used to decorate clothing.

▽ The Serpent Mound earthwork winds 1,300ft along a hilltop in southern Ohio. It may have been built as a sacred image.

Trading links across North America
Raw materials used by the Adena and Hopewell peoples came from far-flung communities:
Stone from various areas for making tools, weapons, and tobacco pipes.
Copper and silver from the Great Lakes for making jewelry and musical instruments.
Mica from the Appalachian Mountains for making cutouts, shaped like hands, claws, and snakes.
Obsidian from the Rocky Mountains, a glass-like rock for making knives and spearheads.
Shells and alligator teeth from the Gulf of Mexico for making necklaces.
Pottery from south of the Appalachians.

ceremonies. Others are burial mounds, each containing log tombs where the dead were buried with a rich array of beautiful objects. These grave offerings include necklaces, bracelets, and ear ornaments made of gold, silver, copper, pearls, and shell. There are also polished stone tobacco pipes in the form of people or birds, stone and copper tools, and mysterious shapes cut from sheets of copper and mica.

Trading networks
The objects found in the burial mounds were made by skilled craftsmen from rare and precious materials. Many of these materials came from great distances, imported through a network of trade routes stretching hundreds of miles along rivers and tracks from the Great Lakes to the Gulf of Mexico.

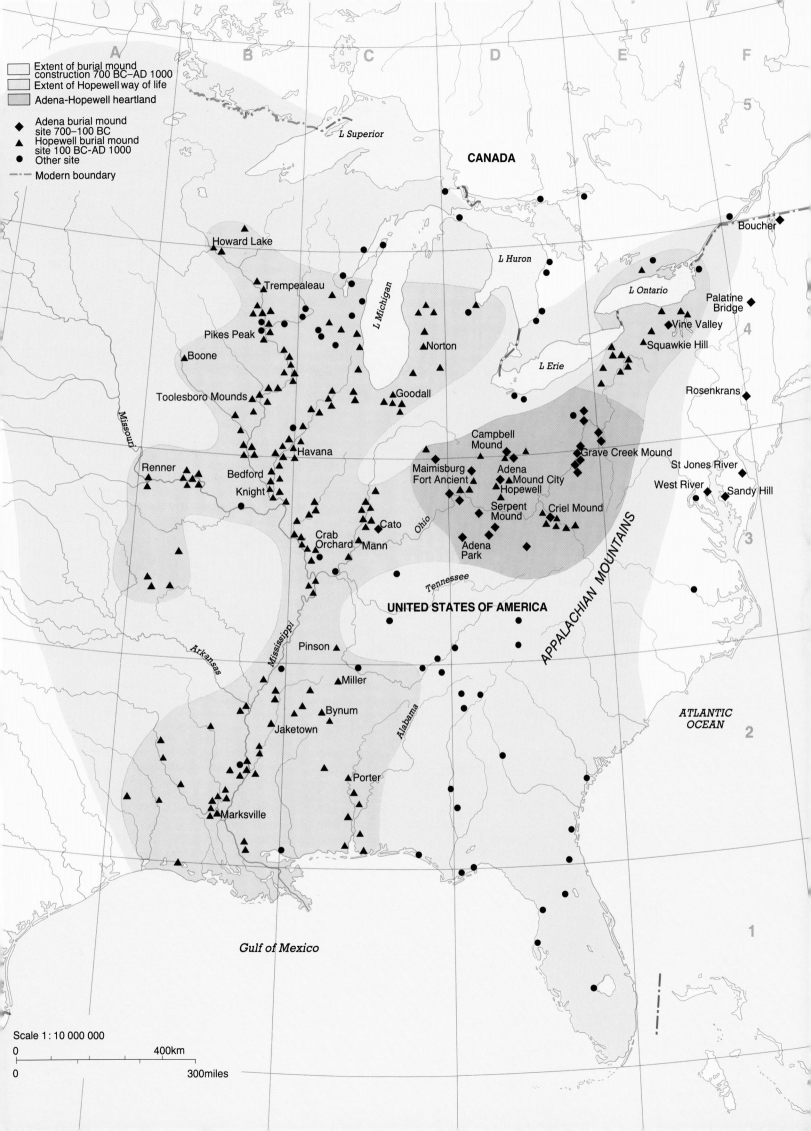

Legend

- Extent of burial mound construction 700 BC–AD 1000
- Extent of Hopewell way of life
- Adena-Hopewell heartland

◆ Adena burial mound site 700–100 BC
▲ Hopewell burial mound site 100 BC–AD 1000
● Other site
–·–·– Modern boundary

Map labels

CANADA

UNITED STATES OF AMERICA

L Superior
L Huron
L Michigan
L Ontario
L Erie

Missouri
Arkansas
Mississippi
Ohio
Tennessee
Alabama

APPALACHIAN MOUNTAINS

ATLANTIC OCEAN

Gulf of Mexico

Site names

Howard Lake
Trempealeau
Pikes Peak
Boone
Toolesboro Mounds
Renner
Bedford
Knight
Havana
Crab Orchard
Mann
Cato
Norton
Goodall
Campbell Mound
Maimisburg
Fort Ancient
Adena
Mound City
Hopewell
Serpent Mound
Adena Park
Criel Mound
Grave Creek Mound
Vine Valley
Squawkie Hill
Palatine Bridge
Boucher
Rosenkrans
St Jones River
West River
Sandy Hill
Pinson
Miller
Bynum
Jaketown
Porter
Marksville

Scale 1 : 10 000 000

0 — 400km
0 — 300miles

TEMPLE MOUND BUILDERS: THE FIRST TOWNS

Around AD 800 Eastern Woodland farmers began to grow a stronger, more productive type of maize imported from Mexico. In some sheltered areas it could be planted and harvested twice in the same season. Better farming methods led to a new and wealthy way of life which is known as the Mississippian.

Mississippian settlements were larger than any built before. With thousands of inhabitants, they are considered the first real towns in North America. A typical town consisted of a number of rectangular flat-topped mounds grouped around a plaza or square. The mounds were built of earth with a ramp or stairway of logs leading to the summit. Temples and houses were built on top.

The Southern Cult
Many objects, such as shell discs and copper sheets engraved with strange designs, have been found in temple mounds in the southern Mississippian area. Designs include crosses, suns, weeping eyes, and hands with an eye in the center of the palm. They seem to be symbols of the Southern Cult, a mysterious religion about which very little is known.

△ A chest ornament, or gorget, made of shell, engraved with a man's head. It may have been a Southern Cult object.

▽ Important people were often buried under the floors of temples built on the flat-topped mounds. Others, as here, were buried in cemeteries near the towns. Grave goods – pottery and shell or copper gorgets – were placed around the bodies.

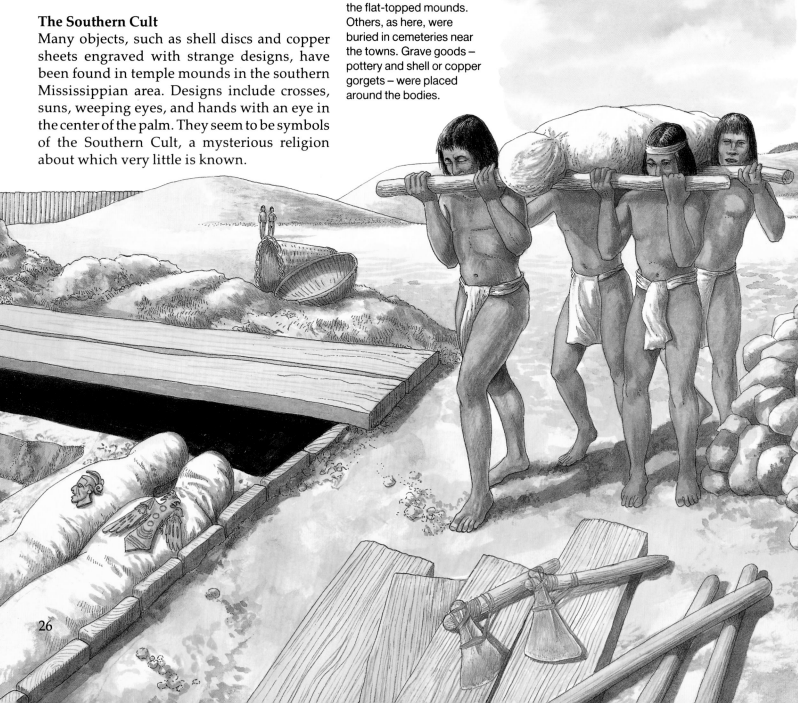

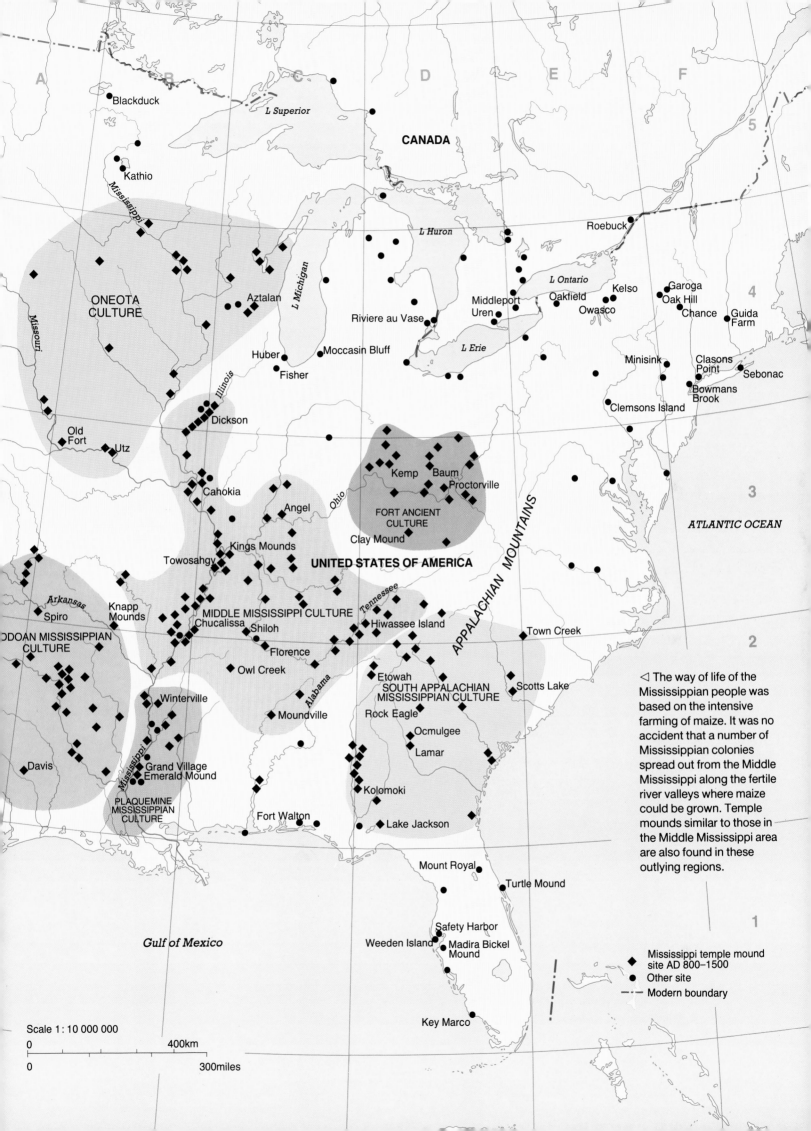

Blackduck

L Superior

CANADA

Kathio

Mississippi

B

C

D

E

F

5

L Huron

Roebuck

ONEOTA
CULTURE

Aztalan

L Michigan

Riviere au Vase

L Ontario

Middleport
Uren

Oakfield

Kelso

Owasco

Garoga
Oak Hill
Chance

Guida
Farm

4

Missouri

Huber

Fisher

Moccasin Bluff

L Erie

Minisink

Clasons
Point

Sebonac

Bowmans
Brook

Illinois

Dickson

Clemsons Island

Old
Fort

Utz

Cahokia

Angel

Ohio

Kemp

Baum
Proctorville

Kings Mounds

FORT ANCIENT
CULTURE

ATLANTIC OCEAN

3

Towosahgy

Clay Mound

UNITED STATES OF AMERICA

APPALACHIAN MOUNTAINS

Arkansas

Spiro

Knapp
Mounds

MIDDLE MISSISSIPPI CULTURE

Chucalissa

Shiloh

Tennessee

Hiwassee Island

Town Creek

2

ODOAN MISSISSIPPIAN
CULTURE

Florence

Owl Creek

Alabama

Scotts Lake

Winterville

SOUTH APPALACHIAN
MISSISSIPPIAN CULTURE

Moundville

Rock Eagle

Etowah

▷ The way of life of the
Mississippian people was
based on the intensive
farming of maize. It was no
accident that a number of
Mississippian colonies
spread out from the Middle
Mississippi along the fertile
river valleys where maize
could be grown. Temple
mounds similar to those in
the Middle Mississippi area
are also found in these
outlying regions.

Davis

Mississippi

Grand Village
Emerald Mound

Ocmulgee

Lamar

PLAQUEMINE
MISSISSIPPIAN
CULTURE

Fort Walton

Kolomoki

Lake Jackson

Mount Royal

Turtle Mound

1

Gulf of Mexico

Safety Harbor

Weeden Island

Madira Bickel
Mound

◆ Mississippi temple mound
   site AD 800–1500

● Other site

–·–·– Modern boundary

Scale 1 : 10 000 000

0   400km

0   300miles

Key Marco

MOUND SITES

Cahokia – Mississippian mound city

Cahokia lies near the modern city of St. Louis. Founded about AD 600, Cahokia was the largest prehistoric city north of Mexico. In its heyday, about AD 1100, as many as 10,000 people may have lived there.

Cahokia contains more than 100 manmade mounds of various shapes and sizes. The largest, Monk's Mound, is a flat-topped pyramid rising in four terraces to a height of 100ft above the surrounding valley. Its builders had no carts or pack animals, but carried the earth there themselves, in baskets.

About 1200 a wooden fence was put up around the central plaza, enclosing Monk's Mound and 16 smaller mounds. Wooden buildings on mounds were probably temples and houses of important people. Some of the mounds contained burials. Smaller mounds

▽ Cahokia consists of over 100 mounds grouped around plazas or squares. Monk's Mound is one of the largest manmade earthworks in North America. It contains over 780,000 cu. yd. of earth, and at its base measures 990 x 660 ft (more than 12 times the area of a modern football pitch).

outside the fence may have been for houses and burials of less important people.

Government and trade
Until its decline in about 1450, Cahokia was probably the seat of government for the surrounding area. Several smaller towns were strung along the banks of the Mississippi and the other rivers that flowed into it near Cahokia. The city was also an important trading center. Grave goods found in burial mounds there include copper items from the Great Lakes, mica from the Appalachians, and shells from the eastern seaboard.

△ ▷ Small hamlets of wattle and daub houses (*right*) were scattered over the fertile river plain around Cahokia (*above*). These were the homes of the farmers who supplied the

city with food. In their fields they grew maize, beans, and squash – a kind of marrow. They stored their surplus crops in pits dug in the ground outside their houses.

△ This pottery bottle modeled in the shape of a mother nursing her child, comes from the Cahokia area. Mississippian pottery in the form of people and various animals may have been a copy of similar pots brought from Mexico by traders.

Emerald Mound, a mound town

Emerald Mound lies in the lower Mississippi valley, near the present-day city of Natchez. It was one of at least nine towns inhabited by the Natchez Indians. French explorers who visited the Natchez in the early 18th century have left descriptions of their way of life. Only a few years after these visits the Natchez were almost completely wiped out by warfare and disease.

The Natchez may have been descendants of the earlier Mound Builders. They were ruled by a powerful chief called the Great Sun. He wore elaborate feather crowns and cloaks and was carried everywhere in a litter. His subjects treated him with great respect. Anyone who displeased him he put to death. When the Great Sun died, his wife and servants were killed and buried with him.

▷ Emerald Mound is a natural hill that was flattened to make a large platform 770ft long and 440ft wide. Two earthen flat-topped pyramids were built on top. The larger one is almost 33ft high.

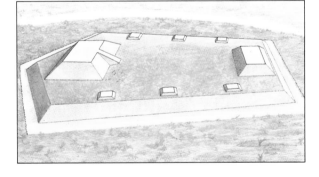

▷ This stone tobacco pipe from Emerald Mound is carved in the form of a crouching man, his arms and legs tightly bound with cords, representing a prisoner. It is over 5in high and 7in long.

Pipes were made for both everyday and ceremonial use. The large size of this pipe probably means that it was used in some kind of ceremony.

The Natchez chief's pipe bearer was one of his most important servants. When the chief died, his pipe bearer was killed and buried with him.

29

THE NORTHERN IROQUOIANS

The Northern Iroquoians lived in woodlands to the northeast of the Mississippian people. By about AD 1000 they had spread over a wide area around the eastern Great Lakes and along the St. Lawrence river valley. When European explorers first met them in the 16th century, they were divided into 12 tribes (see map).

Village life

The Iroquoians were hunters, farmers, and also traders, living in villages set among their fields. In the surrounding woods the men hunted deer, bear, and caribou. They also trapped smaller animals like rabbits and beaver. The women cultivated the fields with hoes and digging sticks. They planted the seeds and tended the young crops. The most important crops were those known as the "three sisters" – maize, beans, and squash. After about 10 or 15 years, the soil became exhausted and the fields had to be abandoned. The men cleared another patch of forest to make more fields and a new village was built nearby.

Early Iroquoian villages were built on the banks of streams or rivers. Later, because of fear of attack from neighboring tribes, villages were often built on hilltops and protected by great wooden palisades in three rows with watchtowers: "...and these they stock with stones in wartime to hurl upon the enemy, and water to put out the fire that might be laid against their palisades." (Gabriel Sagard, who worked among the Huron, a 17th-century missionary).

Villages sometimes formed leagues for war or trade, but there was no central government within a tribe. Each village was ruled by an elected chief with a council to advise him and help him keep order.

Longhouses

An Iroquoian village consisted of a number of longhouses, each one occupied by several related families. Longhouses were built of frameworks of wooden poles covered over with sheets of bark. They varied in size, but one housing 20 families might be 150ft long.

Inside the longhouse, each family had its own section, 13ft long, partitioned off from its neighbors. A row of fireplaces ran along the middle of the floor, one for every two families. Gaps were left open in the roof to allow the

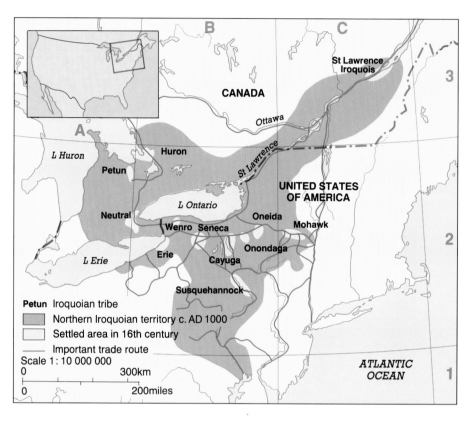

△ The 12 tribes of the Northern Iroquoians. Their territories were around the eastern Great Lakes and along the St. Lawrence valley.

▽ The Mohawk village of Caughnawaga, built about 1690. Earlier villages were larger, with perhaps 50 longhouses occupied by as many as 2,000 people.

This site, west of the Hudson river, is a rare completely preserved Iroquois village and can be easily reached by visitors today.

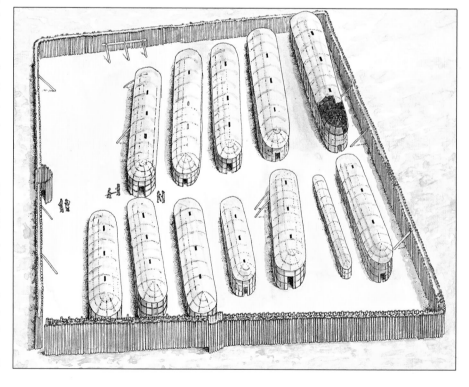

▽ Iroquoian clothing was made from skins and furs obtained in hunting or by trade with other tribes. In warm weather, men, their bodies painted and tattooed as here, wore only a deerskin breechcloth and moccasins. In winter they wore a cloak, long sleeves, and leggings. This male carries a wooden club.

▽ Deer hunting was often a joint activity. Several hundred hunters might band together to drive the deer into a specially built enclosure where they were trapped and immediately killed with spears.

smoke to escape. Food and firewood were stored at one end of the house and in the center there were racks where people kept their belongings – their clothes, hunting weapons, farming tools, baskets, cooking pots and utensils, and birchbark bowls for serving food. Around the walls were low wooden benches covered with skins for sitting or sleeping. In winter people slept underneath the benches for greater warmth.

The fur trade

As traders, the Iroquoians traveled great distances over land on foot or along the rivers by bark canoe. The Huron, for example, traded maize, tobacco, and fishing nets to neighboring tribes, receiving meat and furs in return.

After the arrival of French and English traders in the Eastern Woodlands in the 16th century, the fur trade became very important. In exchange for furs, the traders supplied the Indians with European goods such as beads, cloth, metal tools, and guns. The growth of the fur trade led to fighting among the Iroquoians as different tribes tried to control the trade routes. Many Indians were killed in these wars and many more died of European diseases like smallpox. The Indian population fell so much that when French and English colonists arrived in the Woodlands in the early 17th century, they found vast areas no longer inhabited.

THE GREAT PLAINS

The Great Plains stretch across central North America from the Mississippi river to the Rocky Mountains. In the prehistoric period, up to about AD 1500, most Plains Indians were farmers, living in villages in the eastern prairies. Only a few nomadic buffalo hunters lived in the High Plains to the west (see map).

The eastern prairies

Farmers from the Eastern Woodlands settled the valleys of the Mississippi and its tributaries, and the eastern prairies about 250 BC.

By about AD 900 there were farming villages built on terraces or bluffs along the valleys. Crops were grown in the flood plain below the village. As in the Eastern Woodlands the most important were maize, beans, and squash.

People probably left their villages once or twice a year to go on long hunting trips. Large quantities of buffalo bones have been found at village sites. The main farming tool was a hoe made from a buffalo shoulder bone lashed to a wooden handle.

◁ Typical Great Plains landscape, showing a "buffalo jump." Until Europeans brought horses to America, Indians hunted buffalo and other game on foot. Often hunters banded together to stampede a herd over a cliff, like the one shown here.

The American artist, Paul Kane, reported in the 1840s that:

"... there are thousands of them [buffalo] killed annually ... but not one in twenty is used in any way by the Indians so that thousands are left to rot where they fall."

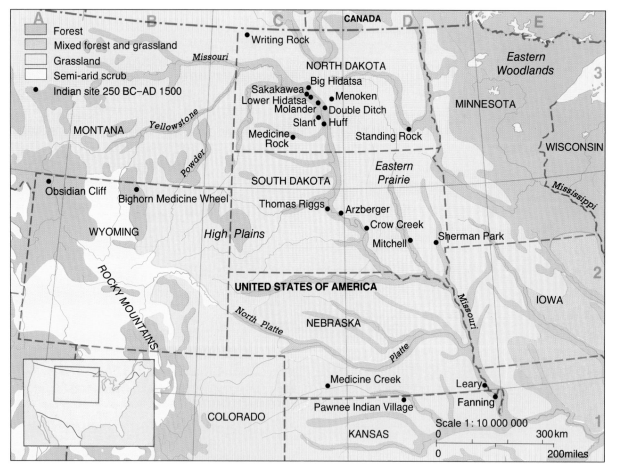

◁ Most of the Plains Indians were farmers before the Europeans arrived. They grew maize and other crops along the river valleys of the eastern Plains. Here the soil was light and easily worked with Indian farming tools like hoes and digging sticks. The richer, heavier soil of the prairies was not cultivated until the arrival of European plows and draft animals. In the western or High Plains there were only a few nomadic Indians who were hunters all the year round.

The High Plains

In the western Plains, the climate was too dry for farming. The 16th century Spanish explorer Francisco de Coronado (see page 10) wrote scathingly of the Plains Indians whom he met that *"they do not plant anything and do not have any houses except of skin and sticks and they wander around with the cows ...."* These were the nomadic hunters who lived in skin tents and followed the buffalo herds on foot. They had few possessions since everything had to be carried on their backs or by their dogs. Dogs were trained to pull a *travois* (a type of sledge).

△ A Pawnee village in the Great Plains. This is in Nebraska, photographed in 1871. Bundles of tipi poles are stacked against the entrance passage to the earthlodge. Pawnee families lived in tipis when they went on their long summer hunting trips.

▷ From the 15th century Plains farmers lived in large dome-shaped earthlodges. Like their earlier houses, these were built of wood covered with turf and earth. Entry was through a covered passage. Inside, there was a central fireplace with a smoke hole in the roof above. Raised wooden platforms running along the wall were used as benches or beds.

Before the reintroduction of the horse, Prairie tribes used dogs for hunting, pulling travois, and carrying lightweight loads.

LIFE ON THE PLAINS

Plains Indians are usually seen as mounted warriors in fringed buckskin and feathered headdresses. But this way of life lasted only for a short time – less than 100 years in fact. The reason that it existed at all was due to the horse. It ended around the 1880s with the European expansion, by horse, across the Plains.

Horses had once lived in America, but they died out about 8000 BC. They were brought back to America by 16th-century Spanish settlers. At first the Spaniards refused to sell horses to the Indians, but the Indians got hold of them by raiding Spanish ranches or capturing strays. By about 1800 most Plains tribes had managed to obtain at least a few horses.

With horses the Indians were able to travel farther and faster than before. Buffalo hunting became an easier and more attractive form of livelihood. More people began to move out into the Plains to become nomadic hunters. These included people like the Sioux, Cheyenne, and Arapaho who had been farmers, and the Cree who had been hunters and trappers in the Eastern Woodlands.

Tribes, tipis, and ceremonies

During the fall and winter the Plains tribes split up into small bands, each with its own chief. In spring the bands left the shelter of their winter quarters and moved out on to the Plains. In summer they all came together, pitching their cone-shaped tents or tipis in one great camp circle.

The Plains tipi was made of buffalo skin stretched over a framework of wooden poles. Inside, a lining of more skins kept out the drafts. Smoke from the central fireplace escaped through an opening at the top which could be opened or closed according to the direction of the wind. The tipi was in fact very well designed for life on the Plains. It was warm in winter and cool in summer. Most important of all, it could be quickly dismantled and packed up when it was time to move camp.

Summer was the time for organizing communal activities and for holding tribal councils and ceremonies. The most important ceremony held at this time was the Sun Dance. This was when people joined together to offer prayers and thanks for supernatural help in times of trouble. It was called the Sun Dance because

◁ Mato-Topé, a Mandan chief by American painter Catlin in 1832. His shirt decorations show that he has scalped (cut the skin and hair of the top of the head off) many enemies. The wooden knife records his killing of a Cheyenne chief in hand-to-hand combat. Mato-Topé, along with most of his tribe, died of smallpox in 1837.

many of those taking part gazed at the sky as they offered their prayers.

Hunting buffalo

The buffalo gave the Plains Indians almost everything they needed. The meat was eaten fresh or dried and stored in bags. The skins, cleaned and dressed, were made into clothing, bedding, tipi covers, bags, and riding tackle. Tools were made from the bones, ropes from the hair, thread from the sinews, cups and spoons from the horns.

Ways of hunting varied with the seasons and the movements of the buffalo. In winter men hunted in small groups, on foot if the snow was deep. Then they might use the age-old method of surrounding a herd and driving it into a corral or over a cliff. When the whole tribe gathered for the summer camp, hundreds of mounted hunters joined together to pursue the buffalo on the open Plains.

◁ Within each tribe there were several men's societies. Their duties included protecting the camp or village and organizing hunting and war parties. Each society had its own dances which it performed on special occasions. The Mandan Bull Society, shown here, danced in spring to lure the buffalo herds closer to the village.

▽ A buffalo hunt, painted by George Catlin in the 1830s. Mounted hunters, armed with lances or bows and arrows, surround a buffalo herd, shooting them down as they mill about in confusion. Fifty years later the buffalo had gone and the Indians were confined to reservations. Painters like Catlin captured this way of life before it vanished forever.

THE FAR WEST

West of the Great Plains, between the Rockies and the Sierra Nevada, lies a vast wilderness of desert and mountain. Here Indian farming methods were not possible. Much of the area was too dry and desolate to support people.

The Great Basin

The southern part of the region is known as the Great Basin. Only small scattered bands of hunters and gatherers lived here. The women foraged among the sparse grass and scrubby bushes for seeds and nuts, which they ground into flour and made into porridge or bread. Large game such as deer were scarce, but the men hunted rabbits, birds, lizards, and rats, as well as small insects, for example grasshoppers and caterpillars.

Their search for food kept them constantly on the move. In summer they lived in flimsy brush shelters on the banks of shallow lakes and streams. During winter they camped in rock shelters or caves in the mountains. At each campsite they left supplies of flour and dried fruit and meat in storage pits ready for their next visit.

The Plateau

To the north of the Great Basin, around the headwaters of the Columbia and Fraser rivers, is the Plateau, an area of grassland and mountains. The Plateau Indians also gathered wild fruit and plants for food. The bulb of the camass lily, closely related to the hyacinth, was one of their most important sources of food.

There was a greater variety of wildlife here

▷ The Pomo Indians of California made baskets like this as gifts and ceremonial offerings, decorating their surfaces with feathers and beads.

▽ Prehistoric sites of California are located mainly on the coast and along rivers.

Life in the Desert West 1000 BC to AD 1800

In the desert basin Seeds and nuts (especially pine nuts) gathered. Digging sticks used to collect roots. Bows and arrows for hunting deer; nets and traps for catching small game. Clothing from skins and plant fibre; cloaks and blankets of twisted strips of rabbit fur.

On the plateau Fish (especially salmon) caught in rivers with spears, nets, traps, and weirs. Bows and arrows for hunting. Baskets for carrying, storing, and cooking. Clothing from skins, fur, and plant fibre.

California AD 500-1800

Seeds and nuts (especially acorns) gathered and ground into flour using mortars and pestles. Shellfish caught, fishing with spears and bone and shellfish hooks along the coast. Bows and arrows for hunting. Round dome-shaped houses with thatched roofs.

Map labels:

WASHINGTON
Ryegrass Coulee
Marmes Rockshelter
Sunset Creek
Weis Rockshelter, Double House Village
Wakemap Mound
Columbia
Five Mile Rapids

CASCADE RANGE
OREGON

UNITED STATES OF AMERICA
Snake
Wilson Butte
IDAHO

Dirty Shame Rockshelter
Nightfire Island
Suprise Valley
Hogup Cave
Great Salt Lake
Tsurai, Patrick's Point
Karlo Site, Tommy Tucker Cave
Lovelock Cave
South Fork Shelter
Danger Cave
Sacramento
Great Basin
Hickson Petroglyph
Newark Cave
UTAH
Kings Beach
NEVADA
Ellis Landing, West Berkeley Mound, Emeryville Shellmound
Gatecliff Shelter
Bryce Canyon
San Joaquin
SIERRA NEVADA
Mammoth Creek
Vermillion Valley
Owens Valley
Rose Spring
Rocky Gap
Colorado
CALIFORNIA
Panamint Valley
Death Valley
PACIFIC OCEAN
Mohave
ARIZONA
Big Sycamore, Little Sycamore, and Deer Canyons
Topanga Canyon, Mulholland
Malaga Cove
Santa Rosa I
Santa Cruz I
Santa Catalina I
San Nicolas I
Pine Valley, Dripping Springs
San Clemente I
MEXICO

Indian site 1000 BC–AD 1800
Modern boundary
Scale 1 : 10 000 000
0   300km
0   200miles

than in the Great Basin. The rivers teemed with fish, especially salmon. Deer, antelope, and mountain sheep were hunted in the northern forests and mountains. Because food was easier to find, the Indians were able to lead a more settled way of life. For part of the year they lived in villages of "earthlodges." In summer they moved to camps at the fishing grounds.

California

Beyond the Sierra Nevada, in what is now California, the land was rich in natural resources. The valleys were full of game and the

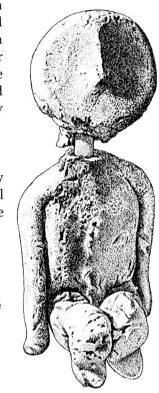

▽ Acorns, the main food of the Californian Indians, were poisonous if not treated carefully. They were first pounded into flour. The flour was then put in a basket and water poured through it to rinse out the harmful acids. The Indians made shelters from brushwood, as here.

▷ The Fremont people lived in Utah between AD 400 and 1300. Little is known about them, but clay figurines like this have been found at their sites.

hills were covered with woods of acorn-bearing oaks. Acorns, the staple diet of the Californian Indians, were pounded into flour in a mortar and boiled with hot stones to make a mushy porridge. The rivers and sea provided many kinds of fish, which the Indians caught with hooks and spears. They prised shellfish from the rocks and hunted seals, dolphins, porpoises, and whales from their canoes.

The rich vegetation made food gathering easier and also provided the women with materials for making mats and baskets. Baskets had many uses. Some were for collecting and storing food. Others were so finely woven that they could hold water, even without being waterproofed with pitch, and these were used for cooking. Baskets made as gifts or for ceremonies were especially beautiful, often covered entirely with brilliantly colored feathers and hung with clamshell beads. Shell beads and feathers were also made into items of jewelry. Elaborate feather cloaks and head-dresses were worn at special ceremonies.

THE SOUTHWEST

The Southwest covers the modern states of Arizona and New Mexico together with southern Utah and Colorado and part of northern Mexico. Although much of the area is desert, there is enough rainfall for farming in some parts at least. Maize has been grown here since about 750 BC. Later crops include beans, squash, and cotton.

The prehistoric Southwest was home to several groups of farmers, for example the Hohokam, the Mogollon, and the Anasazi.

The Hohokam

The Hohokam people settled in the valleys of the Salt and Gila rivers in southern Arizona. They seem to have had many links with Mexico.

Hohokam farmers built a network of canals to draw river water on to the fertile flood plain where they planted their crops. This system of irrigation enabled the Hohokam to grow two

crops a year, one in spring when the river swelled with melting snow and the other in late summer when heavy rain fell.

Their early houses, built of wattle and daub, were set in shallow pits dug in the desert sand. Later they built larger houses of adobe (sun-dried mud brick) entirely above ground. The Great House at Casa Grande is four stories high and has massive adobe walls over 3ft thick.

The Mogollon

The Mogollon people lived in the mountainous region stretching from southern New Mexico and Arizona into northern Mexico. Like the Hohokam, the Mogollon at first lived in pit

▷ This cliff dwelling in central Arizona was built about AD 1200 by the Sinagua people who were farmers in the Verde Valley. It was named Montezuma Castle by early Spanish explorers who thought that it had been built by Aztecs from Mexico.

▷ The Hohokam town of Snaketown flourished from about AD 1 until 1200. The inhabitants dug a system of irrigation canals which carried water from the Gila river to their fields. This allowed them to grow two crops a year instead of only one. In this scene, children play a string game and a man and woman make spear tips beside a stone palette that may have been coated with water and used as a mirror.

houses. After AD 1000 they too began to build large multi-story houses of stone and adobe, often containing 100 or more rooms. These later villages included "kivas," round underground rooms where the men of the village held meetings and performed religious ceremonies.

The Anasazi

The Anasazi were centered on the "Four Corners" area, where the modern boundaries of Arizona, New Mexico, Colorado, and Utah meet. By AD 700 most of the Anasazi had abandoned their earlier pit dwellings in favor of multi-roomed houses of stone and adobe.

In Chaco Canyon in northern New Mexico the Anasazi built huge planned towns like Pueblo Bonito and Chetro Ketl. Here hundreds of rooms arranged on several levels housed many hundreds of people. North of Chaco Canyon at Mesa Verde, villages were at first built on top of the cliffs. But about 1100, for reasons not fully understood, nearly all the villages moved to more sheltered sites in the cliff face. These are the very spectacular cliff dwellings for which the Southwest is now famous (see pages 42-45).

Drought and abandonment

During the 14th century many Southwestern farmers abandoned their towns and villages. Drought and crop failure, perhaps coupled with attacks by nomadic Indians, may have forced them to move to other areas or to seek shelter in neighboring villages.

Their descendants continue to live in Southwestern villages today and many still build terraced houses several stories high. The Pima and Papago Indians are probably descended from the Hohokam, the Zuni from the Mogollon, and the Hopi from the Anasazi.

MIMBRES POTTERY

During the 11th century AD the people of the Mimbres Valley in southwestern New Mexico began to decorate their pottery in a new and interesting way, with a liveliness of design and quality of painting not seen before. Probably, as in modern New Mexico, pots were made and decorated by the women of each village.

Most Mimbres pottery takes the form of shallow bowls painted inside with designs in black and white or in shades of orange and red. Some are painted with geometric patterns such

◁ (*above*) This bowl was found in the grave of a young woman who probably died in childbirth about AD 1100. The design is a clever combination of a bird and a human head.

◁ (*below*) This bowl, like the one above, has a "killing hole" in its base. Here a man seems to be whirling a bull roarer. This is a flat piece of wood or bone attached to a length

of cord. When whirled quickly, it makes a loud roaring noise. It may have been used in ceremonies, perhaps to call up spirits, or bring game, or rain.

40

▽ Mimbres designs often depict strange beings, perhaps taken from myth or legend. This being seems to be part man, part deer, and part bat. He may represent a costumed dancer. In San Juan Pueblo in northern New Mexico, dancers wearing antlers still perform a Deer Dance to ensure a plentiful supply of game for the coming year.

as triangles and zigzags. Others have designs showing human beings and animals including birds and insects. These designs tell us a good deal about the way of life of the people who painted them. They show, for example, deer, mountain sheep, and rabbits which the Mimbres people hunted for food. Sometimes the painting depicts the sort of clothing and jewelry worn. Women, for example, are often shown wearing sandals and a blanket with a fringed sash hanging down behind.

Underfloor burials

Mimbres pottery is often found in burials. The Mimbres people buried their dead under the floors of their houses, even when they went on living above. People were usually buried with various grave offerings, including at least one painted bowl with a punctured base.

"Killing holes" – freeing the potter's spirit

Before the bowls were placed in the grave they were ceremonially "killed." This means that each bowl had a hole punched through the bottom with some kind of sharp instrument. It is possible that this was done to release the spirit or soul of the bowl's maker – since this was thought to be part of the bowl.

▽ Although the bowls themselves were often poorly made, Mimbres potters – believed to be only the women, like this young maiden – took great care with their decoration. They mixed their paints from plants, crushed rocks, and earth. Brushes were made from feathers, twigs, and stems chewed until the ends became soft and flexible. The bowls were not fired in a kiln. Instead firewood was heaped around them and they were baked in a slow-burning bonfire.

Mesa Verde

Mesas – steep-sided hills with flat tops – are typical features of the Southwestern landscape. Mesa Verde is now a national park in Colorado. During the 12th century AD the Anasazi people built huge terraced houses in the shelter of the mesa's overhanging cliffs. These cliff dwellings were in fact large villages, housing hundreds of people.

The people of Mesa Verde were farmers. Traces of their fields and irrigation terraces can still be seen on the flat top of the mesa. Most of the cliff dwellings in Mesa Verde were abandoned early in the 14th century. As elsewhere in the Southwest, this was no doubt due to drought and the failure of the maize harvest. After the cliff dwellers left, the area became the home of nomadic hunters.

Cliff Palace

Of the many ruins in Mesa Verde National Park, the largest and most famous is Cliff Palace. It contains over 400 rooms and its massive walls are four stories high in places. It was not in fact a palace, although its many rooms and stone towers perhaps give it the appearance of one.

The rooms were small, often oddly shaped, and with low ceilings. While some of the rooms had windows and doors, others seem to have been entered through the roof, most likely by a ladder. Some rooms were living quarters, one family to each room. Others were used for storage: probably for food supplies and stocks of seed corn. Yet other rooms may have been for communal milling where the women ground their corn.

There are as many as 23 kivas (see page 39) at Cliff Palace. This is quite a large number and some archaeologists have suggested that Cliff Palace may have been a religious center for all the people of Mesa Verde.

No one is sure what the towers at Cliff Palace were intended for. Were they perhaps lookouts or fortresses against enemy attack ? Or were they observatories for following the position of the sun in order to calculate the best times for planting and harvest ?

Mesa Verde
Canyon de Chelly

Canyon de Chelly

Canyon de Chelly is a national monument in northeastern Arizona. The area is one of mountain ranges cut by steep-sided canyons over 650ft deep. Here, as at Mesa Verde, 12th-century Anasazi farmers built their tall cliff houses in the shelter of the enormous canyon walls. So that they could climb to the top of the canyon, they cut holds for their hands and feet in the sheer face of the cliff.

The Anasazi chose to live here because the canyon floor provided the best farming land in the area. They built their houses in order to have a clear outlook over their fields. There are around 150 cliff dwellings along the 18mi length of Canyon de Chelly. They are built of sandstone blocks cut from the canyon walls. Most are quite small and would have housed perhaps no more than 30 or 40 people at any one time. As well as living accommodation, they also include storage rooms and kivas. Although protected by the overhanging cliffs, most faced south and remained open to the sun. The interiors of the houses were cool in summer and warm in winter.

◁ The ruins of Cliff Palace, seen in winter from the cliff above. Far from being the palace of a ruler, it was in fact home to hundreds of Anasazi farmers and their families. Each family occupied one small room.

The round buildings at the front are kivas (underground meeting rooms), now roofless. When complete, their roofs formed open courtyards for the buildings behind.

▷ The White House, the remains of an Anasazi cliff dwelling, appears almost overwhelmed by the massive walls of Canyon de Chelly. The White House ruin is in fact in two parts. The smaller, upper part is shown here, while 30ft below another cluster of about 45 rooms lies on the floor of the canyon, tucked against the cliff face. These dwellings were not designed to any fixed plan. Their shape depended on that of the caves and niches that sheltered them.

Chaco Canyon

Chaco Canyon lies in an isolated part of northwestern New Mexico, about 95mi south of Mesa Verde. Between AD 900 and 1100 the Anasazi built 12 huge planned towns along the canyon. In these towns hundreds of people lived in multi-story blocks of rooms built of stone and adobe.

The towns were linked to each other and to the outside world by a wide network of roads.

▽ Even in its ruined state today, Pueblo Bonito is impressive. It was called the biggest apartment block in the world until a larger one was built in New York in 1882. Living rooms and kivas (meeting rooms) can be seen ranged around the curving rear wall.

As the building grew, the earliest rooms at the back were completely enclosed. Lacking windows and with entry only through the roof, they were probably used for storage. Living rooms were large with plastered walls. Few seem to have had fireplaces, so cooking was probably done outside on the terraces.

Several very large kivas (see page 39) were sunk into the central plaza. The ceremonies

Traders came, bringing goods from distant places, such as shells from the Pacific coast and copper bells and brightly feathered birds from Mexico. Other goods would have flowed back along these roads, for the towns were full of skilled craftsmen and women – potters, weavers, makers of fine baskets and feather cloaks, carvers of shell, turquoise and jet.

The "pretty village" – Pueblo Bonito
Pueblo Bonito is the largest and also the most spectacular of the Chaco Canyon settlements. Early Spanish explorers were so impressed by its appearance that they gave it its present name – Spanish for "pretty village."

The town faces south towards the Chaco river, with its curving rear wall tucked against the cliffs of the canyon. Its 800 rooms rise in terraces around the central plaza like a vast amphitheater. The roofs of the lower tiers provided open terraces for the rooms above.

▷ In its heyday in the 12th century AD, Pueblo Bonito housed over 1,200 people. The city is in the shape of a huge D, with its round back to the canyon wall. Entrance to the village was by ladder. There were at least 800 rooms, built on several levels.

Roof terraces acted as extra living space and many household activities probably took place in the open. Women prepared meals and made pottery, while men smoked their pipes, wove cotton cloth, and made arrowheads from stone. In the many kivas, ceremonies were held throughout the year to ensure the well-being of the community.

held in these probably involved all the men of the community. There were many smaller kivas scattered among the houses which would have been used by family groups or religious societies.

Fear of attack
Pueblo Bonito seems to have been solidly built for defense. At the front there were no

▷ Chaco Canyon potters specialized in making jugs, bowls, and ladles with decorative geometric designs. Women made the pottery by hand, coiling thin rolls of clay on top of one another. The potter's wheel was unknown in the Americas at this time.

windows on the lowest level, and none in the curving side at all. The original single gateway was first narrowed and then finally blocked up completely. Entry to the town was only by means of ladders which could be pulled up by those inside. It is not clear what sort of attack the inhabitants feared. The Apache and Navajo raiders who ravaged the pueblos (villages) in later centuries had yet to make their appearance in the Southwest.

Abandonment of the towns
The Chaco towns, like Anasazi settlements elsewhere, were dependent on agriculture. Farmers irrigated their crops by collecting rainwater and channeling it to their fields. This, however, was not enough to save them from the droughts which affected the Southwest during the last quarter of the 13th century. Crops failed and the whole Chaco Canyon way of life began to collapse. By the early 14th century, the inhabitants had moved away to other areas and these once thriving centers were left deserted.

HOPI RITUAL DRAMA

The Hopi still live in eight villages or pueblos perched on three mesas in northern Arizona. Like their Anasazi ancestors, who inhabited this area over 1,000 years ago, they are farmers. And in much the same way as the Anasazi did, the Hopi continue to plant their crops of maize, beans, and squash.

Because the Hopi live in a dry, semidesert area where farming is difficult, they give great importance to performing complicated rituals designed to bring rain and produce good harvests. The average Hopi man probably spends almost half his time either preparing for or taking part in dances and ceremonies.

Seasonal ceremonies and dancing

The annual round of ceremonies begins in November with Wuwuchim, which celebrates the creation of the world. The various religious societies hold their ceremonies in the kivas.

From December until July the "kachinas" (see below) dance and sing in the plaza to bring good fortune to the village. They are supernatural beings who are impersonated by masked dancers. All the parts, even those of female kachinas, are taken by men.

In mid-August the Flute or Snake societies perform ceremonies to bring rain. Finally, in September and October, the women's societies dance to welcome the harvest.

The kachinas

The kachinas are very important to the Hopi. There are over 300 of them, all different. They can be recognized by their painted masks and brightly colored costumes. Some are the spirits of tribal ancestors. Others are animal spirits or natural forces, such as rain, wind, cloud, and thunder.

In February the kachinas visit Hopi villages for Powamu, the bean planting ceremony. Led by the Kachina Mother, they enter the village at dawn. They run among the spectators, handing out gifts and receiving food in return. The clown kachinas entertain the crowd with their acrobatic skills, jokes, and games. The Niman ceremony in July marks the kachinas' return to Kachina Village, their distant mythical home in the mountains. They will not be seen again until December when they return to celebrate the winter solstice.

Children were encouraged to learn kachina dances by copying them. Their play-acting was seen by American archaeologist, J. Fewkes:

About 15 boys and girls, no more than 15 years of age, took part, each dressed in a ceremonial kilt and blanket; their bodies were painted and feathers were tied in their hair....and they danced and sang as do their elders....Some of the children were carried into the kivas in the arms of their fathers to prevent them from slipping from the ladders. (at Walpi Pueblo, 1900)

▽ Ogre kachinas visit Hopi villages in February for the bean planting ceremony. They threaten to carry off naughty children unless they are given presents of meat and corn meal.

▷ Wooden dolls, carved and painted to represent kachinas, are given to Hopi children so that they can learn more about the ceremonies in which the kachinas appear.

▷ Two clown kachinas photographed at the bean planting ceremony at a Hopi village in 1893. In the background stand Kachina Mother and an ogre kachina. (Taking photographs at any Hopi ceremonies was forbidden in 1911.)

▽ Unmarried girls, in their cotton mantles, and other villagers gather to watch and listen to the all-male Flute Society dancing and singing in the plaza. Every other year in August Flute and Snake society members perform ceremonies to bring rainclouds.

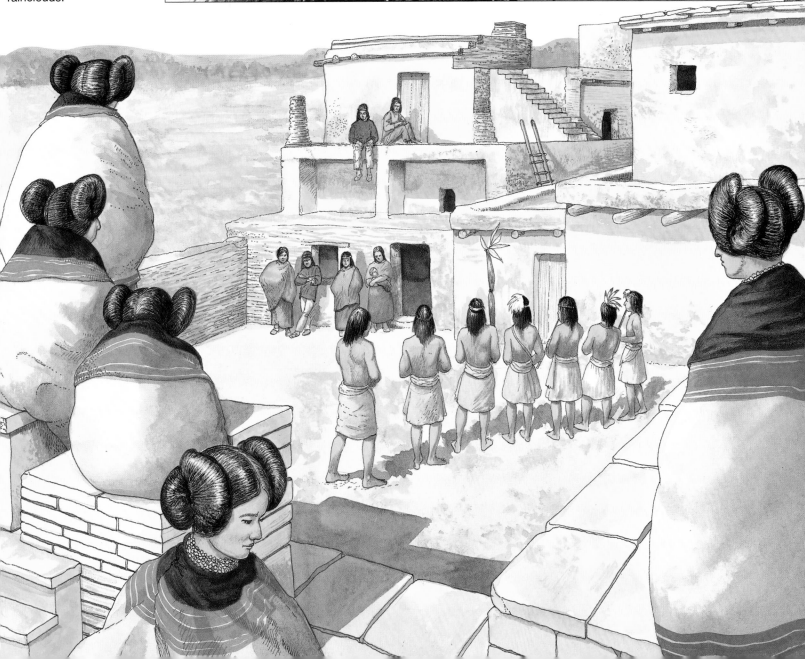

NORTHWEST COAST

The Pacific Coast, stretching from southern Alaska to northern California, is a rugged strip of land with many small islands, deep inlets, and narrow beaches. In many places high mountains rise abruptly from the shore and dense forests of spruce, cedar, and fir grow all the way up to the water's edge.

Living off the sea and forests

The sea, rivers, and forests gave the Indians almost everything they needed. As well as abundant supplies of fish and shellfish, there were several kinds of whales, seals, sea lions, and porpoises. The forest provided raw materials for making houses, canoes, weapons, tools, boxes, and bowls. Baskets, mats, and even clothing were woven from strips of bark.

Ancient settlements and houses

Hunters and fishermen first inhabited this region 10,000 years ago. About 1000 BC the way of life typical of the Northwest Coast began to appear. It was a way of life that lasted until the 19th century almost without change. Like their 19th-century descendants – the Kwakiutl, Haida, Tsimshian, Tlingit, and others – prehistoric Indians lived for most of the year in villages along the coast. Although they sometimes went inland to gather berries or to hunt deer and bears, they were first and foremost fishermen.

Villages consisted of large rectangular houses, built of wooden planks. Each house was occupied by several related families, numbering perhaps 30 or 40 people in all. Every family had its own living area in the house, separated from that of all its neighbors by wooden screens or woven mats.

Carving in wood – totem poles

Woodworking was an important industry and Indian craftsmen used a variety of specialized tools. Hammers, adzes, chisels, awls, and drills were made of stone, bone, and shell before the Indians obtained metal from traders and European settlers. Sadly, wood decays quickly in the damp Northwest Coast climate. Most surviving woodcarvings date only from the 19th century or later.

Perhaps the best known wood carvings are totem poles. These were made for a variety of

▷ This mask was worn by a Kwakiutl dancer taking the part of Bowkus, a wild being who lured the spirits of drowned people to his home in the woods.

▽ High mountains cut the rocky Pacific coast off from the interior. Here a warm wet climate has produced a land rich in natural resources.

Glacier Bay
Stikine
ALASKA
Alexander Archipelago
BRITISH COLUMBIA
Dodge Island
COAST MOUNTAINS
Queen Charlotte Islands
Natalkuz Lake
Tezli
Potlatch
Namu
ROCKY MOUNTAINS
ALBERTA
CANADA
Fraser
Nesikep Creek
Milliken
Esilao
Stselax
Vancouver Island
Marpole
PACIFIC OCEAN
Hoko River
Ozette
USA
WASHINGTON
Wakemap Mound
Columbia
Netarts Sand Spit
COAST RANGE
Five Mile Rapids
OREGON

● Indian site 3000 BC–AD 1800

Scale 1 : 10 000 000

0   300km
0   200miles

reasons. Some displayed the emblems of the families who owned them, rather like coats of arms. Some were put up to commemorate important events or as memorials to the dead. Others were house posts built on the fronts of houses, with doorways cut in their bases.

Masked dancers and trick masks

Carved and painted wooden masks were (and still are) used in dances and ceremonies. Many were worn in dances which acted out legends of ancestors and family origins. Performances were often very dramatic. Masked dancers might sometimes appear suddenly through trap doors or swing through the air on ropes to give the illusion of flying.

The masks worn usually depicted strange supernatural beings with whom ancestral heroes had come into contact. These beings often appeared in the form of animals or birds. When a dancer put on a mask, he took on the personality of the spirit that it represented.

There were many different types of masks. Among the most elaborate were those known as "transformation" masks. By pulling hidden strings, the wearer of this kind of mask could open it up to reveal another, quite different mask within. Some of these masks were so heavy that the dancer had to wear a special harness strapped to his body.

△ Although this wood Bella Coola mask appears to be a human face, the style of its painted pattern indicates an animal spirit.

◁ A totem pole put up to make fun of a white trader who cheated Indians. Even in his absence, his face, carved at the pole's top, could be jeered at.

▽ Many masks were worn in dances that acted out myths and legends. These told of ancestral heroes and their adventures with supernatural beings, who took the form of animals or terrifying monsters. The wearer of this Nootka bird mask could make it seem more realistic by opening and closing its beak.

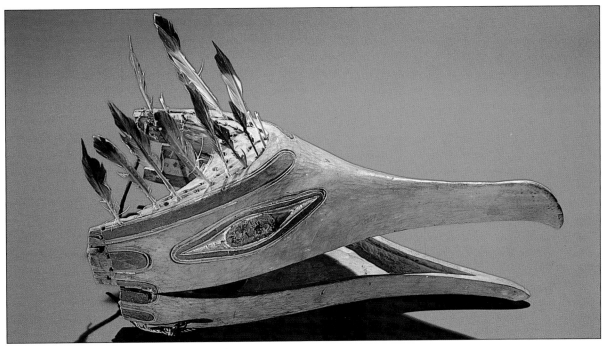

PART TWO

THE HISTORY OF LATIN AMERICA

△ A stylized human being on a painted bowl from Panama. The design shows stronger influences from South America than from North.

▷ A view of Machu Picchu in Peru, showing its complex structure, varied stonework, and dramatic setting.

LATIN AMERICA : CLIMATE AND VEGETATION

Latin America consists of those areas where Spanish or Portuguese (two languages that are derived from Latin) are spoken. The areas are Mexico, the countries of Central and South America, and the Spanish-speaking Caribbean islands (see map page 9).

Stretching southwards from the United States border to the cold and stormy waters of the south Atlantic, Latin America has enormous variations in both climate and landscape.

Mexico and Central America

Much of Central America has a tropical or subtropical climate, though in the north and in Mexico there are deserts and dry grasslands. Hurricanes sweeping in from the Atlantic Ocean often batter the coastline. In the southern lowlands areas of swamp and tropical forest result from a heavy seasonal rainfall.

South America

Amazonia, the name given to the great Amazon river basin, covers more than 2,800,000 sq. mi. (almost the size of Australia). It is a vast area of rainforest ("selvas"), the home of scattered Indian groups. They lived by clearing small patches of forest to grow crops before moving on. They had little impact on the forest which soon recovered. Now, however, vast areas are being cleared for commercial purposes and the rainforest is being destroyed forever.

North and south of the rainforest there are drier tropical areas of grassland called "llanos" or "campos." Farther south lie the hot dry scrubland of the Gran Chaco and the rolling grasslands known as the "pampas." To the south, from Patagonia, the land becomes increasingly cold and bleak. Cape Horn at the tip of Tierra del Fuego is famous for its storms.

▽ Circular terraced slopes in the southern highlands of Peru show how people have changed the landscape to suit their needs. In the mountains there are few broad valleys where crops can be grown, but Inca farmers created flat fields by cutting these step-like terraces down the steep hillsides. The terraces are supported by stone walls and stone steps led from one level to the next. Drainage channels carry water from terraces on the upper slopes to those many feet lower down.

▷ The great range of natural vegetation in Latin America is shown on this map. For example, in the hot and steamy Amazon jungle – the world's greatest rainforest – the rainfall averages 60 – 100in each year. By contrast, the Atacama Desert, along the coasts of Peru and northern Chile, receives almost no rain.

The Amazon, together with its great network of tributaries, meanders across much of Brazil and eight other countries. The Amazonian rainforest is now being lost at a rate of 2 per cent – the size of Belgium – each year.

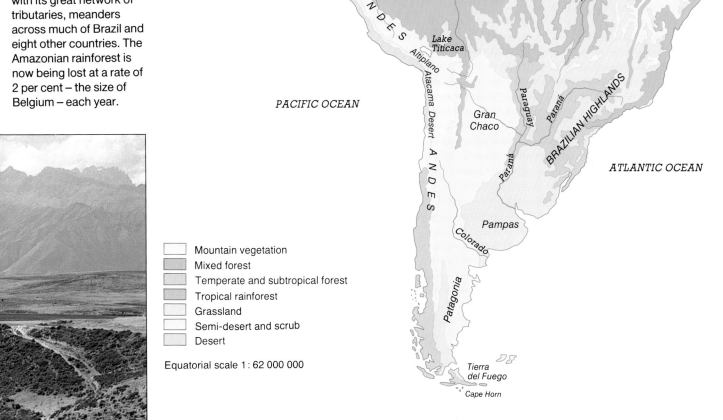

Gulf of Mexico

Sierra Madre Occidental
Sierra Madre Oriental
Yucatán
Isthmus of Tehuantepec
Cuba
Greater Antilles
Jamaica
Hispaniola
Lesser Antilles
Caribbean Sea
Lake Nicaragua

Galapagos Is

Orinoco
Llanos
GUIANA HIGHLANDS
Japurá
Ucayali
Selvas
Amazon
Madeira
Araguaia

A N D E S
Altiplano
Lake Titicaca
Atacama Desert

PACIFIC OCEAN

Gran Chaco
Paraguay
Paraná
BRAZILIAN HIGHLANDS
ATLANTIC OCEAN

Paraná
Pampas
Colorado

Patagonia

Tierra del Fuego
Cape Horn

Mountain vegetation
Mixed forest
Temperate and subtropical forest
Tropical rainforest
Grassland
Semi-desert and scrub
Desert

Equatorial scale 1 : 62 000 000

◁ The area around Lake Titicaca (left), at some 13,200ft above sea level, is bleak and often very cold. Yet people have lived here for more than 10,000 years. In sheltered areas, maize and cotton have been grown, and around the lake shores people fished and hunted water birds and deer.

53

MESOAMERICA AFTER THE ICE AGE

By Mesoamerica we mean the parts of Mexico and Central America that were civilized before the Spanish Conquest. In Mesoamerica, as elsewhere, the ending of the Ice Age brought changes in the climate and landscape, at least in the highlands of central and southern Mexico. As the climate became drier and warmer, grasslands turned into deserts. The herds of large grazing animals, like mammoth, mastodon, horse, and giant bison, disappeared, leaving smaller game such as rabbits and deer for people to hunt. The Indians learned to adapt to changes in their environment by developing new hunting methods and tools, especially those for grinding seeds and nuts.

In fact, hunting may not have been particularly important in this area. People may have concentrated as much, if not more, on collecting wild plants for food. Mesoamerica has always been rich in plant food. Even the desert areas produce edible plants such as mesquite, cactus, and agave.

Beginnings of farming – the Archaic period

The change from gathering plants to growing them for food took place over thousands of years. The period during which this change took place is known as the Archaic period. We can only guess how the change came about. Maybe, to save time and effort, people decided to plant extra supplies of their favorite food where they could be sure of finding it. The

▽ In the Archaic period people moved from nomadic hunting and gathering to farming and village life. The earliest evidence for the growing of maize comes from dry cave sites in Tamaulipas and Tehuacan.

The farming villages that appeared during the Formative period (from around 2000 BC) tended to flourish in more humid areas like the Pacific and Gulf Coasts, the Maya lowlands and the fertile highland valleys of Oaxaca and Mexico. There were also elaborate ceremonial centers from this time. Improved strains of maize and other crops were grown in several areas.

The Archaic period c. 7000-2000 BC

c.7000 BC Nomadic hunters grew crops like squash and chili peppers near campsites.
c.5000 BC Maize grown in Tehuacan Valley.
c.3000 BC Villages of pithouses (partly underground dwellings, with wattle and daub sides) formed.
c.2300 BC People begin to make pottery.

The Formative period c.2000 BC to AD1 (central Mexico) and AD290 (Maya highlands)

c.1200 BC Rise of Olmec civilization.
c.400 BC Zapotec city of Monte Alban founded.
c.AD 150 Rise of the city of Teotihuacan.

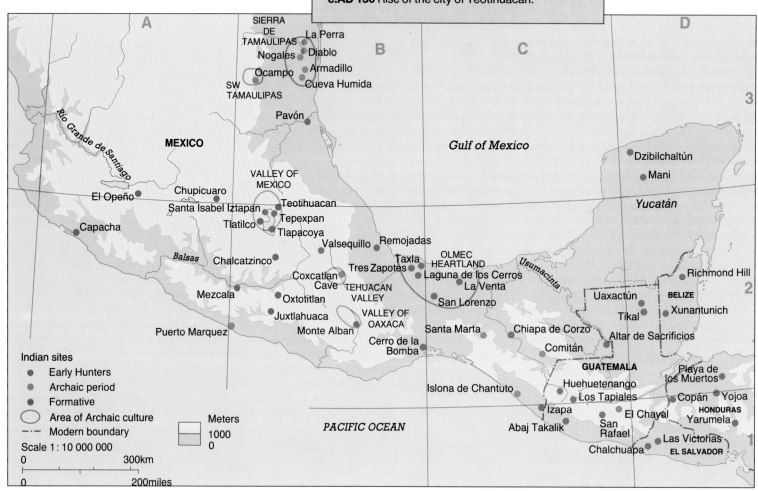

Indian sites
- Early Hunters
- Archaic period
- Formative
- Area of Archaic culture
- Modern boundary

Scale 1 : 10 000 000

Meters
1000
0

0   300km
0   200miles

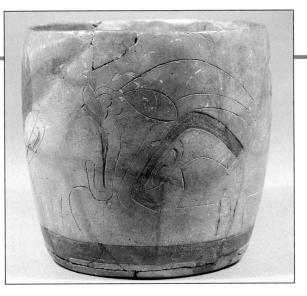

▷ Pottery bowl from Tlapacoya in the Valley of Mexico, 1200-900 BC. The design engraved on this bowl shows the head of a supernatural being with a snarling mouth. Coiling was the usual way to make pottery in Mesoamerica. Sometimes a previously made pot was used as the mold for a new one.

earliest cultivated plants would have looked no different from wild ones. Then, as people began to select seed from the best plants to sow the following year, bigger and more productive varieties developed.

Not all plants grown at this period were for food. Archaeologists studying early plant remains have found that one of the first to be cultivated was the bottle gourd. It was not good to eat, but, when hollowed out and dried, it made an excellent storage container.

The Tehuacan Valley

One of the areas where people began to make the move from gathering food to farming crops and animals is the Tehuacan Valley in the modern Mexican state of Puebla. This is a semidesert region about 6,600ft above sea level. For thousands of years small bands of nomadic hunters and gatherers camped in the caves and rock shelters here. The remains of the food they ate have been preserved in the dry conditions.

From about 7000 BC, as well as gathering seeds, nuts, and berries, they began to grow plants such as squash, avocado, chili peppers, and cotton. By around 5000 BC they were also growing maize. Most probably similar changes were taking place all over Mesoamerica, but in wetter areas, like the tropical lowlands, plant remains have not survived so well.

Gradually people came to rely more and more on the food they grew themselves. They began to make special tools and equipment, like grinding stones to crush maize and stone bowls in which to store their seeds. They no longer needed to travel far in search of food and they began to settle down. The first village found in the Tehuacan Valley dates from 3000 BC.

Early villages – the Formative period

Around 2300 BC people began to make their jars and bowls from pottery rather than stone. Since pottery is too fragile to be carried around between campsites, it seems that by this time most people were living in villages built near their cultivated plots of land.

During this Formative period, settled village life became the rule rather than the exception, with villages and small towns of thatched houses found all over Mesoamerica.

△ Scrub landscape near the Coxcatlan Cave in the Tehuacan Valley, an early maize-growing area.

▽ 5,000 years of farming changed the wild maize cob (*left*) to the modern maize cob (*right*). The earliest cobs from the Tehuacan Valley were only 1in long and were used for food and making beer.

OLMEC CIVILIZATION

The Olmec heartland lay in the tropical forests and swamps of the modern Mexican states of Veracruz and Tabasco. The origins of Olmec civilization remain mysterious, but it probably arose from farming settlements that flourished in the fertile river valleys.

From around 1200 BC the Olmec began to build important ceremonial centers. These had earth mounds and carved stone monuments. The main centers are at San Lorenzo, La Venta, Laguna de los Cerros and Tres Zapotes.

Impressive stonework

The Olmec made colossal stone carvings, from monuments to powerful human heads, and also finely worked jade axes, figurines, and pendants. These are all the more remarkable because the Olmec had no metal tools. All carving must have been done with chisels and grinding tools made of stone – a slow process.

Apart from the huge stone heads, thought to portray individual rulers, most Olmec carvings are of strange and terrifying supernatural beings. They are often drawn from creatures of the tropical forest and coast, which the Olmec knew and feared – the jaguar, snake, cayman (a kind of alligator), harpy eagle, and shark. Most important – and perhaps most terrifying – was a half human, half animal "were-jaguar," often shown as a howling baby with the sharp fangs and angry eyes of a snarling jaguar.

Beyond the heartland – Olmec trade

The Olmec had to look far across and even beyond their heartland to obtain many of their

△ Olmec sculpture ranged from objects small enough to be held in the hand, like this tiny lifelike jade bust, to the huge stone heads over 7ft high which have been found at San Lorenzo and La Venta.

raw materials. Massive basalt boulders from the Tuxtla Mountains were brought to La Venta, perhaps floated downriver by raft.

The same trade routes also carried Olmec civilization to other areas. Olmec objects, or objects in the Olmec style, have been found all the way from central Mexico to Costa Rica. Although, for reasons still unknown, the power of the Olmecs faded around 400 BC, they influenced the later great civilizations.

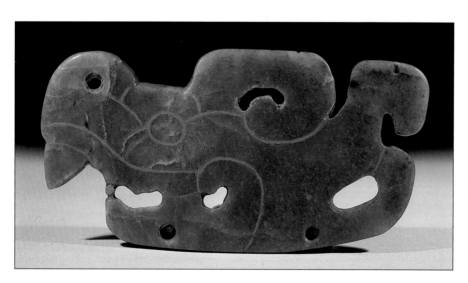

◁ Many Olmec carvings depict strange and even fearsome supernatural beings. This jade carving from Guatemala is of the Shark God.

▷ The warm, wet climate of the Olmec heartland produced rich farming land, where maize and other crops could be grown all year round. But many of the raw materials needed by the Olmecs had to be obtained through trade with other areas outside the heartland.

El Mesón ▲

Nestepe ▲

Tres Zapotes ■

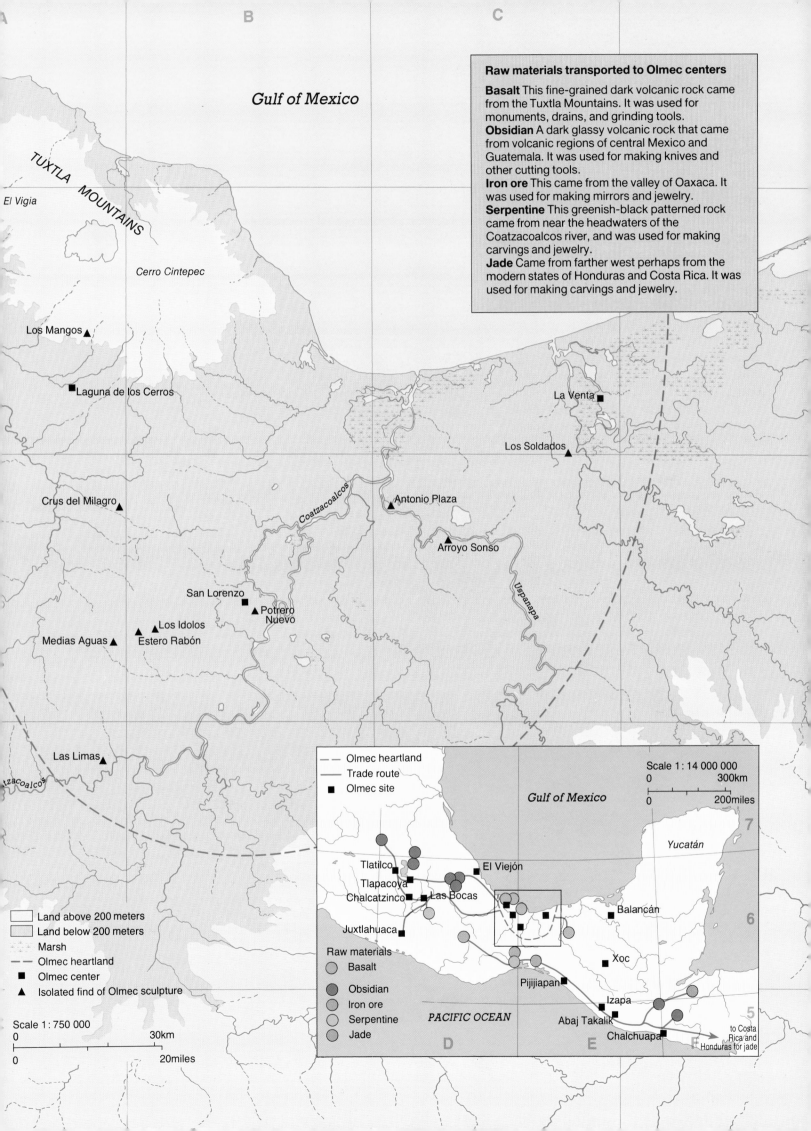

Gulf of Mexico

TUXTLA MOUNTAINS

El Vigia

Cerro Cintepec

Los Mangos ▲

■ Laguna de los Cerros

La Venta ■

Los Soldados ▲

Crus del Milagro ▲

Antonio Plaza ▲

Arroyo Sonso ▲

Coatzacoalcos

Uspanapa

San Lorenzo ■

▲ Potrero Nuevo

Los Idolos ▲

Medias Aguas ▲   Estero Rabón ▲

Las Limas ▲

atzacoalcos

Raw materials transported to Olmec centers

Basalt This fine-grained dark volcanic rock came from the Tuxtla Mountains. It was used for monuments, drains, and grinding tools.
Obsidian A dark glassy volcanic rock that came from volcanic regions of central Mexico and Guatemala. It was used for making knives and other cutting tools.
Iron ore This came from the valley of Oaxaca. It was used for making mirrors and jewelry.
Serpentine This greenish-black patterned rock came from near the headwaters of the Coatzacoalcos river, and was used for making carvings and jewelry.
Jade Came from farther west perhaps from the modern states of Honduras and Costa Rica. It was used for making carvings and jewelry.

Land above 200 meters
Land below 200 meters
Marsh
Olmec heartland
■ Olmec center
▲ Isolated find of Olmec sculpture

Scale 1 : 750 000
0   30km
0   20miles

Olmec heartland
Trade route
■ Olmec site

Scale 1 : 14 000 000
0   300km
0   200miles

Gulf of Mexico

Yucatán

Tlatilco

El Viejón

Tlapacoya

Chalcatzinco   Las Bocas

Balancán

Juxtlahuaca

Xoc

Raw materials
Basalt
Obsidian
Iron ore
Serpentine
Jade

Pijijiapan

Izapa

PACIFIC OCEAN

Abaj Takalik

Chalchuapa

to Costa Rica and Honduras for jade

A   B   C   D   E   F

7   6   5

SAN LORENZO

The Olmec ceremonial center of San Lorenzo was built on a 165ft high, partly natural, partly manmade plateau. On the summit nearly 200 earthen mounds grouped around rectangular courtyards remain. These were probably the bases on which houses were built. Larger mounds nearby may have been the bases for temples. The actual buildings, made of wood and thatch, have long since disappeared. A series of artificial pools was probably used for ceremonial bathing. An overflow system consisted of U-shaped sections of basalt drains laid end to end and fitted with lids.

The people of San Lorenzo

At its peak San Lorenzo probably contained around 1,000 people, the most important members of the community – rulers, nobles, and priests. Another 2,000 or so people may have lived in the surrounding area, in farming hamlets on the plain below the plateau. Around 900 BC San Lorenzo was violently destroyed. The stone sculptures were deliberately smashed and their remains buried. People continued to live there for a time but no more monuments were put up.

LA VENTA

La Venta consists of a group of earthen mounds and enclosures built on an island in the swamps of northern Tabasco. After San Lorenzo was destroyed, La Venta was the Olmec's main political and religious center.

The largest mound at La Venta is the so-called Great Pyramid (over 100ft high and 420ft across its base). To its north lie a series of lower mounds and courtyards. Burials with rich grave goods have been found under some of the mounds, but no one has yet excavated the Great Pyramid itself.

Ceremonial buried offerings

The ceremonies performed here included the burial of offerings. Among the objects found are mirrors of highly polished iron ore and axeheads, necklaces, and figurines carved from jade, serpentine, and granite. Perhaps most spectacular are three mosaic pavements each made up of 485 serpentine blocks and representing the face of a jaguar.

Around 400 BC La Venta was destroyed. Its monuments were brutally defaced, just as at San Lorenzo 500 years earlier. What led to this terrible destruction remains a mystery.

▷ These figurines of jade and serpentine were found buried underneath a floor at La Venta. They had been arranged as if to show some kind of ceremony. They may be priests marching in procession or captives being brought before a ruler. About 100 years after they were buried, someone cut a hole in the floor above to inspect them. Their hiding place must have been carefully recorded as the hole is directly over them.

▽ There are several of these large flat-topped basalt blocks at La Venta. Although often described as altars, they may have been used as thrones. The figure here, seated cross-legged in the niche, holds a rope which leads round the corner of the block to a bound prisoner.

△ This colossal stone head from San Lorenzo is one of a number found there and at La Venta. It may be a portrait of an Olmec ruler. It is carved from a basalt boulder brought 50mi from the Tuxtla Mountains to the north of San Lorenzo.

Teotihuacan – "Place of the Gods"

About 30mi northeast of Mexico City lie the ruins of Teotihuacan. Built around AD 150, it was the greatest of all the ancient American cities but who the inhabitants were is still not known. Over 8 sq. mi of temples, palaces and houses were laid out on a rectangular grid pattern, and perhaps 200,000 people lived there. For 600 years the city dominated the Valley of Mexico. Through trading links, its power spread over much of Mesoamerica.

A great north-south roadway, the Avenue of the Dead, crosses the center of Teotihuacan. Ruins of over 75 temples line its route. Gods known from later civilizations were depicted in temple carvings and paintings – Tlaloc the Rain God, Chalchihuitlicue the Water Goddess and Quetzalcoatl the Feathered Serpent. The largest and oldest building in the city is the Pyramid of the Sun. It was built over a cave, which may have been a sacred place.

A great center of craft and trade

There were hundreds of workshops scattered throughout the city. Skillful craftsmen made tools and weapons of obsidian or carved ornaments from shell and jade. Others made pottery, from heavy cooking pots to fine vases and incense burners. These goods found their way to other areas beyond Mesoamerica.

In return, merchants brought turquoise back from southwestern North America, shells and copal incense from the Gulf coast, and quetzal feathers from the lands of the Maya. Merchants from Teotihuacan may have settled in Maya cities, setting up trading posts and perhaps marrying into local families.

Around AD 750 large areas of the city were destroyed by fire. There are no written records to tell what happened. But the city's greatness was not forgotten. Aztec emperors made pilgrimages there.

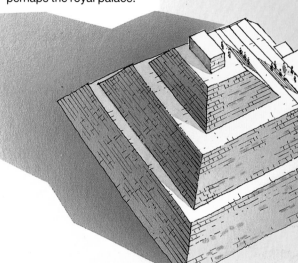

◁ The Pyramid of the Sun as it is now. Rising to a height of more than 200ft, it towers over the city and can be seen from afar.

▷ The Pyramid of the Sun as it looked in its heyday. To the left is the smaller Pyramid of the Moon, marking the northern end of the Avenue of the Dead. Beyond the Pyramid of the Sun (not shown here) lay the city's market place and the Ciudadela, a walled enclosure with the Temple of Quetzalcoatl and perhaps the royal palace.

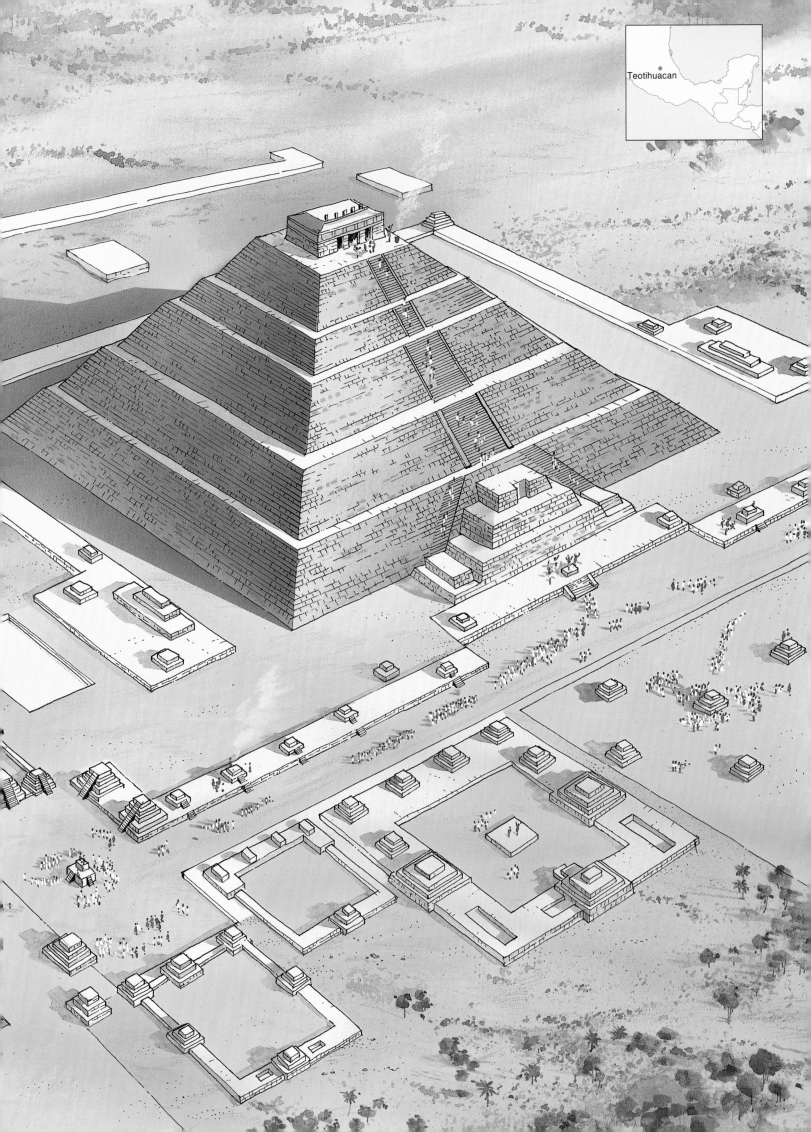
Teotihuacan

MAYA CIVILIZATION

The Maya was undoubtedly the greatest of ancient American civilizations. Probably it was from the Olmecs that the Maya learned the systems of writing and recording time which they later perfected. As well as their scientific achievements, the Maya are famous for great stone-built cities with towering temple-pyramids, and palaces. Many of these cities have been reclaimed from the jungle and restored to some of their former glory.

City-states and warrior kings

Maya cities were independent states, each with its own ruling dynasty. Rulers, usually male, passed succession from father to eldest son. They claimed descent from the gods and inscribed their ancestry on monuments or walls.

The city-states were constantly at war – not to gain territory, but to take prisoners. Important ceremonies, such as a ruler's accession to the throne, included the offering of a human sacrifice to the gods for which a supply of prisoners was needed.

Time and astrology

Because ancestry was important, the Maya needed a system of recording time. Their system is known as the Long Count. A date was calculated by counting up the number of days that had elapsed since a fixed starting point. For reasons unknown, this starting point corresponds to 3114 BC in our calendar.

The Maya had two calendars. One was of 365 days, divided into 18 months of 20 days each, with an extra five days at the end. The other was a sacred calendar consisting of 260 days, divided into 13 weeks of 20 days. It was used to foretell the future and avoid bad luck. Only priests trained in astrology could read the sacred calendar and people consulted them before important events. So, if a child was born on an unlucky day his naming ceremony could be put off until a luckier one.

△ Abandoned for five centuries, the great temple-pyramids of Tikal rise above the jungle. The largest Maya city, Tikal is famous for its splendid stone architecture. In the 8th and 9th centuries AD, 50,000 people may have lived here.

Numbers and Calendars

The Maya used three basic symbols for numbers : a stylized shell for zero, a dot for one and a bar for five, (4 dots = 4, 2 bars and a dot = 11 and so on). Time was recorded in units of 144,000 days (baktun), 7,200 days (katun), 360 days (tun), 20 days (uinal) and 1 day (kin). Each of these calendar units was represented by a different glyph (picture symbol – see also pages 64-65).

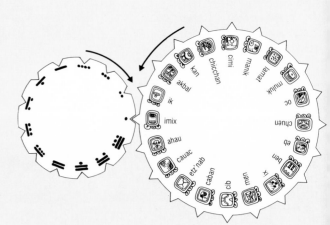

positional values		
	x 144 000	baktun
	x 7200	katun
	x 360	tun
	x 20	uinal
	x 1	kin

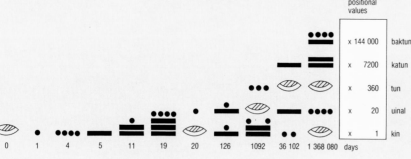

0	1	4	5	11	19	20	126	1092	36 102	1 368 080	days

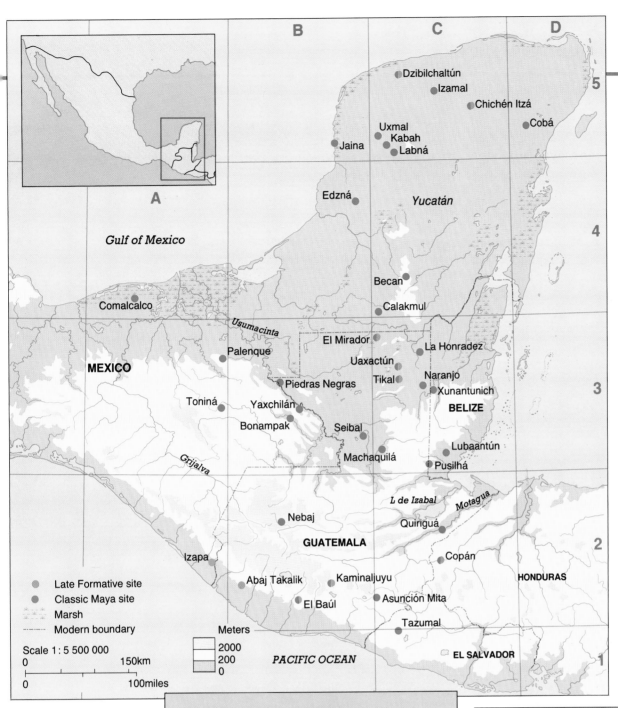

B   C   D

5

Dzibilchaltún
Izamal
Chichén Itzá
Uxmal
Kabah   Cobá
Labná
Jaina

Edzná   *Yucatán*

4

Gulf of Mexico

Becan

Calakmul

Comalcalco

Usumacinta

El Mirador   La Honradez
Uaxactún
Palenque   Naranjo
Piedras Negras   Tikal
Xunantunich
MEXICO   **BELIZE**   3

Toniná   Yaxchilán

Bonampak   Seibal
Lubaantún
Machaquilá   Pusilhá

Grijalva   *L de Izabal*   *Motagua*

Nebaj   Quiriguá

GUATEMALA   2

Copán

Izapa   **HONDURAS**

Abaj Takalik   Kaminaljuyu

El Baúl   Asunción Mita

Tazumal

Meters   **EL SALVADOR**   1

○ Late Formative site
● Classic Maya site
░ Marsh
–·– Modern boundary

Scale 1 : 5 500 000

0   150km
0   100miles

PACIFIC OCEAN

2000
200
0

◁ For over 500 years
Maya civilization flourished
in three regions: in the
highlands of Guatemala;
in the low-lying tropical
rainforests of northern
Guatemala and Belize; and
in the Yucatán peninsula.
Most cities were
independent states
although their rulers were
often linked by marriage.

▽ The Maya did not have
an alphabet. They wrote in
pictures or "glyphs." Most
Maya inscriptions concern
important events in the
lives of Maya rulers.

The scene shown here is
carved on a stone lintel at
Yaxchilán. The top and
middle glyphs tell how on a
certain day Bird Jaguar,
the ruler of Yaxchilán, took
two important prisoners.
The prisoners' names are
written on their thighs.

Calendar

This diagram shows how
the sacred 260-day
calendar worked. The
wheel on the left has 13
numbers. The wheel on the
right has 20 named days.
The wheels turn so that
each number fits in with a
day. The week starts on
1 imix. The next day is 2 ik
and so on. After 13 days
the left-hand wheel comes
round to 1 again to begin a
new week. This time it
starts on 1 ix.

The Maya c. 300 BC to AD 1541

300 BC to AD 300 Early Maya people influenced by
outposts of Olmec civilization at Izapa, Abaj
Takalik, El Baúl, and Kaminaljuyu. Ceremonial
centers built at sites in the southern lowlands such
as Tikal, Uaxactún, and El Mirador.
AD 300-800 The golden age of Maya civilization.
Architecture, art and science flourish at great cities
like Copán, Quiriguá, Naranjo, Piedras Negras,
Uxmal, Cobá, and Chichén Itzá.
AD 800-900 Mayan civilization in the southern
lowlands collapsed, for reasons unknown. Many
cities were abandoned.
c. AD 980 Toltecs invade Yucatán and make
Chichén Itzá their capital. The Maya civilization
survives under Toltec rule.
AD 1200-1500 New Maya capital at Mayapan.
Decline of Maya civilization.
AD 1517-1541 Spanish conquest of Guatemala
and Yucatán.

(on) 7 Imix 14 Tzec   "captor of"   u bac
"the captive of"
chucah "(he) was captured"
Bird Jaguar
Jeweled Skull   second captive   Lord of Yaxchilán

Palenque

Palenque was the most westerly of the Maya city-states. It lies in the modern Mexican state of Chiapas among the wooded foothills overlooking the coastal plain that stretches to the Gulf of Mexico.

Until AD 600 Palenque was small and unimportant. In 615 a new ruler came to the throne. His name was Pacal and he was only 12 years old at the time of his accession. During his long reign and those of his two

▽ The ceremonial center at Palenque with the Temple of the Sun in the foreground. The Temple of the Inscriptions is in the center. (Stone panels have hieroglyphs telling the story of the life of Pacal whose tomb lies at the base of the pyramid.) The palace is on the right.

◁ The palace at Palenque was built over a period of about 100 years. The tower was probably used by astronomers as an observatory. It may also have been a watchtower because, from the top story, reached by a narrow stairway, it is possible to survey the whole plain to the north.

sons (Chan-Bahlum and Kan-Xul II), the city became large and powerful and a center of government for the surrounding area.

Pacal's tomb

Palenque contains many fine buildings, richly decorated with painted plasterwork or stucco. One of the most splendid is the Temple of the Inscriptions. It is set on top of a nine-tiered pyramid built by Pacal to house his own tomb. According to Maya mythology the underworld had nine levels and the nine tiers of the pyramid probably represent this.

Stone panels in the temple are carved with long hieroglyphic inscriptions relating to Pacal's life and ancestry. His astronomers calculated the dates of mythical events going back many thousands of years.

Pacal died in 683 at the age of 80. He was buried in a stone sarcophagus underneath the base of the pyramid. The scene carved on the

sarcophagus lid shows him entering the underworld. The painted stucco panels that decorate the tomb walls depict the nine Lords of the Night who ruled the underworld.

The Palenque palace

The city continued to grow during the reigns of Pacal's sons. Several new temples were built. The palace was enlarged and the graceful four-story tower, unique in Maya architecture, was added. The palace had its own water supply, brought from the nearby Otulum river in a stone-lined aqueduct.

The palace may have been a ceremonial center rather than a royal residence. Stone carvings and decorative moldings (stucco) on the walls show some of these ceremonies. Some celebrate the accessions of rulers and give an idea of the luxury of court life. Others, like the row of captives along a staircase wall, are a reminder of the Maya's warlike nature.

△ This mosaic jade mask perhaps portrays Pacal himself. It was found lying on his sarcophagus.

▷ Glyphs were sometimes shown in human or animal form. This glyph is part of a date incribed on a wall at Palenque. The god of zero (=0) is on the left with the Monkey God representing day on the right. Thus the glyph reads "zero days."

THE TOLTEC EMPIRE

The Toltecs were wise. Their works were all good, all perfect, all wonderful, all marvellous; their houses beautiful, tiled in mosaics, stuccoed, smoothed, very marvellous... they were thinkers, for they originated the year count, the day count; they established the way in which the night, the day, would work.

Here is the Aztec view of the Toltecs, written down after the Conquest by a Spanish priest, Bernardino de Sahagún. Perhaps not surprisingly, the Aztecs, including their Emperor, claimed descent from Toltec ancestors !

The origins of the Toltecs

Although the Aztecs looked back to the time of the Toltecs as a golden age of peace and prosperity, this does not always fit in with what archaeologists have found. Far from being peace-loving, the Toltecs seem to have been fierce and warlike. They ruled by force over much of central Mexico in the 11th and 12th centuries and often fought among themselves.

The origins of the Toltecs are mysterious. They seem to have been a mixture of different groups. From the rocky desert of northern Mexico came the Tolteca-Chichimeca, barbarian nomads who lived by hunting and gathering and perhaps a little farming. The other group, the Tolteca-Nonoalca, came from farther south. Some writers think that they may have been sculptors and craftsmen, brought in to help build the city of Tula.

Tula – The Toltec capital

Tula was built in a commanding position on a high ridge about 40mi northwest of modern Mexico City. Its most impressive building is the four-tiered temple pyramid (archaeologists call it Pyramid B).

Visitors to the temple in its heyday first passed through a colonnaded hall, decorated with relief carvings of marching warriors. They entered the temple itself through a doorway flanked by stone pillars in the form of Feathered Serpents (see page 60). The temple roof was supported on the heads of four colossal stone warriors.

At the temple and in other parts of the city there were strange stone figures known as Chac Mools. These take the form of warriors lying on

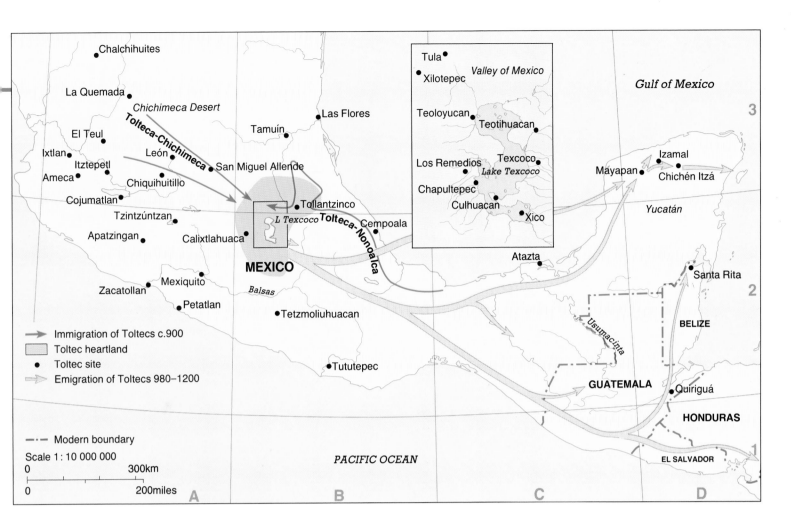

△ The Toltecs were a mixture of nomadic tribes from the Chichimeca Desert and Nonoalca people from the modern state of Oaxaca and the Gulf Coast. During the 10th and 11th centuries AD they spread into many parts of Mesoamerica.

◁ One of four colossal stone figures that once supported the roof of the temple on Pyramid B. It is over 13ft high and consists of four sections of basalt pegged together. It is carved in the form of a Toltec warrior armed with a shield, spear, and spearthrower (called an *atlatl* in Mesoamerica).

▷ This almost lifesize clay figure represents Xipe Totec, the god of vegetation and planting. At springtime ceremonies he was impersonated by a priest wearing the flayed (stripped) skin of a human sacrificial victim.

Rise and decline of the Toltecs

c. 900 Chichimeca nomads enter Valley of Mexico.
c. 950 They join with the Nonoalca people from the south to found the city of Tula.
c. 1000 The Maya city of Chichén Itzá was taken over by foreigners, perhaps Toltecs from Tula (according to Maya texts).
1168 Tula destroyed by Chichimeca invaders.
c. 1200 Power of Chichén Itzá declines. The Maya build a new capital at Mayapan.

their backs. Bowls carved on their chests were probably for sacrificial offerings.

Many things in Tula point to the Toltec's warlike nature. Besides the painted reliefs and statues of warriors, there are carvings of skulls and crossbones, serpents swallowing skeletons, eagles devouring hearts, and prowling jaguars and coyotes. (These last three were symbols of the elite corps in Aztec times.)

The destruction of Tula

In AD 1168 Tula was attacked by fierce nomads who, like the Toltecs themselves, came from the northern desert. The temples and palaces were looted and the great stone warriors hurled to the ground. The inhabitants fled, leaving Tula deserted and in ruins.

Chichén Itzá

According to Aztec legend, the Toltec city of Tula was at first ruled by a wise and peace-loving king named Topiltzin Quetzalcoatl. But the warlike god Tezcatlipoca challenged his authority by witchcraft and he was forced to flee from the city. With his followers, the king set sail across the Gulf of Mexico on a raft made of serpents, promising that he would come back one day to reclaim his kingdom.

The Toltecs in Yucatán

The first Bishop of Yucatán, Diego de Landa, wrote in the mid 16th century:

It is believed among the Indians that with the Itzas who occupied Chichén Itzá, there reigned a great lord named Kukulcan...They say that he arrived from the west...he was regarded in Mexico as one of their gods and called Quetzalcoatl; and they also considered him a god in Yucatán on account of his being a just statesman.

The most impressive building in Chichén Itzá is the Castillo ("castle" in Spanish) which stands in the center of the main plaza. It is in fact a temple pyramid, dedicated to Quetzal-coatl. Excavations in the 1930s found that the Castillo had been built over an earlier temple pyramid. Some people have suggested that this first pyramid may house a royal burial.

Sacred Cenote – the "Well of Sacrifice"

From the main plaza a causeway leads to the Sacred Cenote, a natural well dedicated to the rain god. Pilgrimages to the well continued long after the Spanish Conquest. Offerings dredged from its depths around 1900 spanned a period of over 1,000 years. These offerings included copal incense, carved jade, and gold discs embossed with battle scenes. Bones, too, were recovered, showing that offerings to the rain god included human sacrifice.

The Great Ballcourt

A ballgame, *tlachti*, was played all over Mesoamerica. Two opposing teams played

▽ View across the main plaza at Chichén Itzá, with a jaguar throne standing in the foreground. In the background rises the Pyramid of Kukulcan or Quetzalcoatl, generally known as the Castillo. It is built in 9 tiers with a staircase on each side.

◁ A small carved jade plaque, one of many thousands of objects dredged up from the Well of Sacrifice.

▽ This stone sculpture shows a human face emerging from the gaping jaws of an animal. It may represent a high-ranking warrior wearing a wooden helmet carved in the form of a jaguar. Both Toltec and Aztec warriors wore helmets of this type.

with a large solid rubber ball in a specially made court. The earliest courts date from Olmec times. The Great Ballcourt at Chichén Itzá is the largest of all the known ballcourts. The playing area is 160yd long and 40yd wide, about the area of a modern football field.

The game seems to have been a kind of basketball. The object was to knock the ball through a stone ring set high on the court wall. At Chichén Itzá this must have been especially difficult since there the rings are about 26ft above the floor of the court.

Players were not allowed to touch the ball with their hands, only with their hips and knees. They wore protective clothing, including a heavy belt made of wood and leather, and leather hip-pads, knee-pads, and gloves. Even so, the game was so rough that players were often injured or even killed.

Spectators flocked to the ballcourt to cheer on their favorite team and place bets. These could be enormous: *"gold, turquoise, slaves, rich mantles, even cornfields and houses..."* (de Sahagún – see page 66). But the game was not simply a test of strength and skill. For the players it could be, quite literally, a contest to the death. Carvings around the walls of the Great Ballcourt at Chichén Itzá show members of the winning team sacrificing a defeated opponent by cutting off his head.

▷ With its four-tiered pyramid and colonnades, the Temple of the Warriors at Chichén Itzá closely resembles Pyramid B at Tula (see pages 66-67). The rows of columns are carved on each side with warrior figures.

The entrance to the temple, at the top of the steps, is guarded by a reclining Chac Mool figure, flanked by two Feathered Serpents, the symbol for Quetzalcoatl.

THE AZTEC EMPIRE

The Aztecs claimed to be descended from nomadic barbarians from northern Mexico. Their wanderings were guided by their tribal god Huitzilopochtli whose image they carried with them. About AD 1300 they came to Lake Texcoco in the Valley of Mexico. Already there were powerful city-states here. For a time the Aztecs worked as serfs for some of the rulers.

In 1345 the Aztecs settled on some swampy

The Aztec empire AD 1345-1521

1345 Aztecs found Tenochtitlan on Lake Texcoco.
1428 Triple Alliance formed (Texcoco, Tenochtitlan, and Tlacopan). Aztecs control Valley of Mexico.
1440-1468 Emperor Montezuma I expands empire to the Gulf of Mexico.
1486-1502 Emperor Ahuizotl expands empire to the Pacific Coast and the borders of Guatemala.
1519 Spanish invaders land in Mexico.
1520-21 Emperor Montezuma II killed. Aztec empire destroyed.

▽ By 1502 the Aztec empire was at its full extent. Tlaxcallan and Teotitlan stayed independent states. Conquered provinces had to pay an annual tribute, or tax, to the empire such as clothing and food or luxury goods – jaguar skins and quetzal feathers.

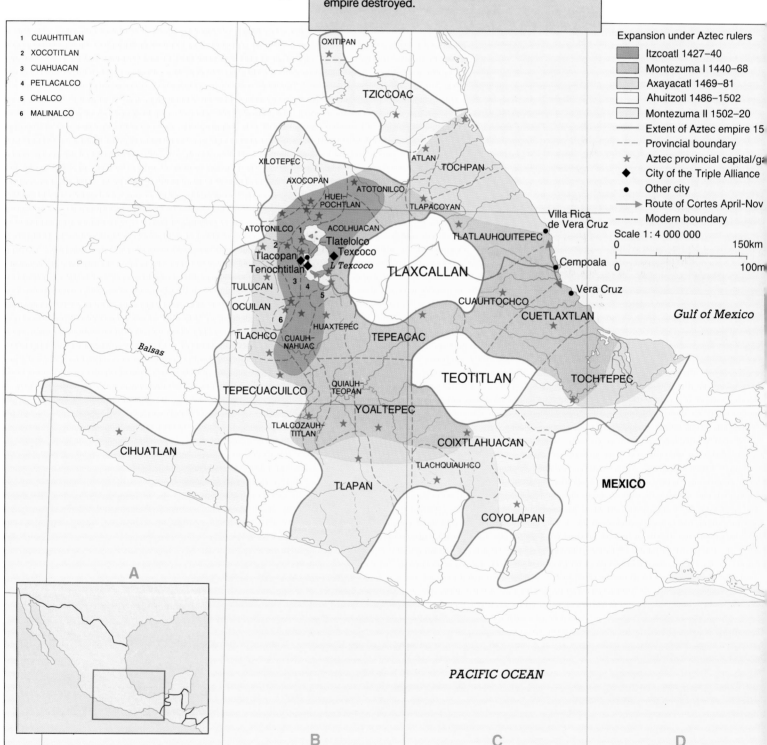

1 CUAUHTITLAN
2 XOCOTITLAN
3 CUAHUACAN
4 PETLACALCO
5 CHALCO
6 MALINALCO

Expansion under Aztec rulers
Itzcoatl 1427–40
Montezuma I 1440–68
Axayacatl 1469–81
Ahuitzotl 1486–1502
Montezuma II 1502–20
Extent of Aztec empire 15
Provincial boundary
★ Aztec provincial capital/ga
◆ City of the Triple Alliance
● Other city
→ Route of Cortes April-Nov
Modern boundary
Scale 1 : 4 000 000
0   150km
0   100m

islands near the western shore of Lake Texcoco. A tribal prophecy had foretold that they would one day build a great city where an eagle, holding a snake, perched on a prickly pear cactus. The Aztecs believed these islands to be the place. On land reclaimed from the swamp they built houses of cane and thatch with a temple for their god. They called the settlement Tenochtitlan (*"place of the prickly pear cactus"*).

The Aztecs came to power by serving as mercenaries for the neighboring city-state of Atzcapotzalco. They became so strong and experienced in war that in 1428 they were able to defeat Atzcapotzalco and take control of its territories. By forming the Triple Alliance (see map) they extended their power over the whole Valley of Mexico. By 1500 the Aztecs controlled an empire of some 10 million people that stretched from coast to coast and from the Valley of Mexico to Guatemala.

▷ A priest impersonating Xipe Totec, god of planting (a Toltec god whom the Aztecs adopted). He wore the flayed skin of a sacrificial victim for 20 days. The shedding of the skin symbolized the sprouting in spring of a new shoot from the husk of an old seed.

The Aztec army

The Aztecs won their vast empire by war, with a large, well organized and well-equipped army. Like a modern army, it was divided into units under the command of officers or war chiefs.

Officers were appointed entirely on merit. Some were elected by those they commanded. Others won their rank by taking captives in battle. The Aztecs needed captives, even in peaceful times, for sacrifice to the gods. The so-called "Flowery Wars" were arranged with other states to obtain such captives.

All boys over the age of 15, except those intending to be priests, trained as warriors. The army's main weapon was the spear and spear-thrower or *atlatl*, but slings and bows and arrows were also used. Most fearsome of all was the *macahuitl*, a flat wooden club edged with razor-sharp blades of obsidian.

Every warrior wore a tunic of quilted cotton and carried a shield of the same material over a cane frame. High-ranking warriors, like the Jaguar or Eagle knights, wore carved wooden helmets and animal skin or feather costumes.

▽ The skull of a captive chosen to impersonate the supreme god Tezcatlipoca ("Smoking Mirror") for one year. During that year the captive was treated with great honor and reverence. When the year was up he was killed as a sacrifice to the god.

The emperor

The Aztec emperor was elected from members of the royal family by a council of nobles, priests and warriors. His actual title was Tlatoani, meaning "Speaker." Because of the records kept by the Spanish invaders, the emperor about whom we know most is the last one, Montezuma II. People treated him like a god. No one was allowed to look directly at his face. Even great nobles had to enter his presence barefoot and with bowed heads. He traveled in a litter carried on the shoulders of his nobles. If he walked, they swept and then covered the ground with cloths so that he need not touch it.

THE AZTEC CAPITAL

When we saw so many cities and villages built both on the water and on dry land... we could not resist our admiration... because of the high towers, cues [pyramids] and other buildings, all of masonry, which rose from the water. Some of our soldiers asked if [it] was not a dream.

With these words Bernal Diaz, a soldier with Cortes (see page 12), recalled his first enchanted glimpse of Tenochtitlan in 1519. Built on swampy islands in Lake Texcoco, it had become a wealthy and powerful city of over half a million people. There were towering temples and palaces, bustling markets, and suburbs of houses and gardens. Produce was grown on chinampas or "floating gardens."

▽ Aztec nobles and warriors survey the ceremonial center of Tenochtitlan. The temple of Quetzalcoatl is before them and beyond it the great double temple pyramid dedicated to Huitzilopochtli, the God of War, and Tlaloc, the Rain God. Nearby is the *tzompantli* or skull rack, where the heads of sacrificial victims were put on display. In the distance are groups of houses and gardens.

The great market at Tenochtitlan

Canoes thronged the lake and the city's network of canals, bringing goods and produce from all over the empire to the great market. Each day more than 60,000 people came to trade. Stallholders offered food and clothing of all kinds, pottery cups and dishes, tobacco pipes, and cigarettes. There were luxury goods – gold, silver, jade, and feathers. Slaves were displayed for sale in wooden cages.

Most people bartered what they had for what they wanted. The Aztecs had no money, but there were some fixed units of value, ranging from cocoa beans (small change) to high-value woven mantles (cloaks) or jade necklaces (one mantle was equal to 100 cocoa beans).

▷ This knife with its sharp stone blade may have been used in sacrificial ceremonies. The wooden handle, inlaid with shell and turquoise, is in the form of an eagle warrior.

The Aztecs paid homage to the gods by making them many kinds of offerings. The most important offering was human blood. The Aztecs believed that, unless the gods were given this "food", the world would come to an end.

THE ANTILLES, COLOMBIA AND VENEZUELA

The Indians who came to greet the explorer Christopher Columbus when he landed in the Bahamas in 1492 were the Arawak. Columbus noted in his log-book :

I gave some of them red caps and glass beads which they hung round their necks, also many other trifles. These things pleased them greatly and they became marvellously friendly to us.

The Arawak were fishermen and hunters, who traveled among the Caribbean islands in large canoes. They were also farmers and grew manioc, maize, beans, and peppers in the fields near their villages of round thatched houses. They also grew cotton, from which they made

▽ Lake Guatavita in the mountains of Colombia, near Bogotá. The Muisca Indians believed it to be the home of a powerful god. Muisca rulers, covered in gold dust, sailed out into the lake to throw in offerings of gold and jewels. This was the origin of the legend of El Dorado ("the Gilded One").

Many gold objects have been dredged from the lake, but it has never been successfully drained. The cut through the hill on the far side of the lake was part of a scheme to drain it in the 1580s. Gold and jewels were recovered, but this attempt was stopped when the cut collapsed, killing many workmen.

◁ △ Carved stone figures found near the mountain village of San Agustín, southern Colombia. Over 300 of these figures are scattered over a wide area.

Some stand alone or in groups on hillsides. Others have been found in stone tombs. Many depict half human, half jaguar beings with bared fangs.

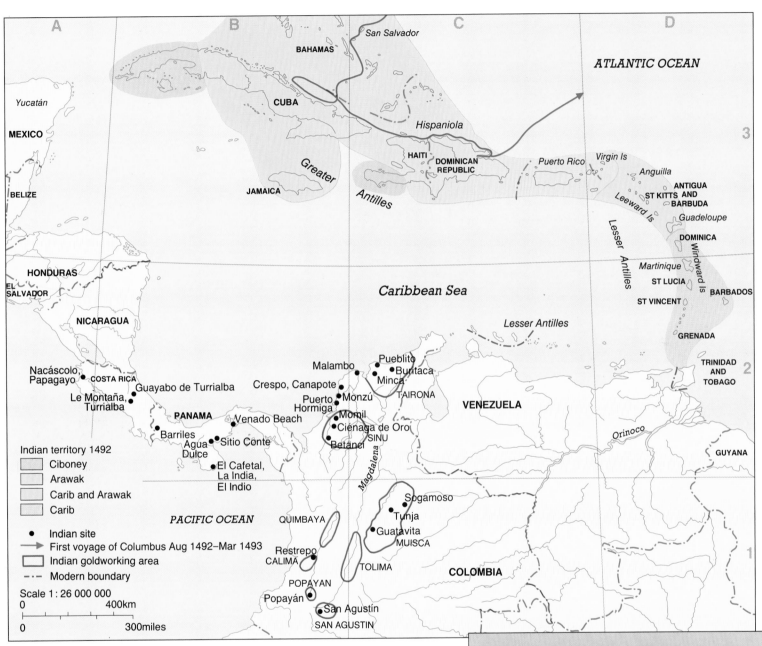

The map includes the following labels:

A
Yucatán
MEXICO
BELIZE
HONDURAS
EL SALVADOR
NICARAGUA
Nacáscolo, Papagayo
COSTA RICA
Le Montaña, Turrialba
Guayabo de Turrialba
PANAMA
Barriles
Agua Dulce
Sitio Conte
Venado Beach
El Cafetal, La India, El Indio

B
BAHAMAS
CUBA
JAMAICA
Greater Antilles
Crespo, Canapote
Malambo
Puerto Hormiga
Monzú
Momil
Ciénaga de Oro
SINU
Betanci
QUIMBAYA
Restrepo
CALIMA
POPAYAN
Popayán
San Agustín
SAN AGUSTIN

C
San Salvador
Hispaniola
HAITI
DOMINICAN REPUBLIC
Puerto Rico
Pueblito
Buritaca
Minca
TAIRONA
Caribbean Sea
Lesser Antilles
VENEZUELA
Magdalena
Orinoco
Sogamoso
Tunja
Guatavita
MUISCA
TOLIMA
COLOMBIA

D
ATLANTIC OCEAN
Virgin Is
Anguilla
ANTIGUA AND BARBUDA
ST KITTS
Leeward Is
Guadeloupe
DOMINICA
Windward Is
Martinique
ST LUCIA
BARBADOS
ST VINCENT
GRENADA
TRINIDAD AND TOBAGO
GUYANA
Lesser Antilles

Legend:
Indian territory 1492
Ciboney
Arawak
Carib and Arawak
Carib
● Indian site
→ First voyage of Columbus Aug 1492–Mar 1493
▭ Indian goldworking area
–·– Modern boundary
Scale 1 : 26 000 000
0   400km
0   300miles

PACIFIC OCEAN

cloth and the hammocks in which they slept.

There were other Indians in the Antilles when Columbus arrived. The Ciboney, the earliest inhabitants, were by then few in number, having been largely driven out by the Arawak. More threatening to the Arawak were the Carib, a fierce warlike people who had the reputation of being man-eaters.

The friendliness that had marked the first meeting between the Indians and Columbus was not to last. In under 100 years the Arawak had vanished from the Caribbean islands, victims of European disease and warfare.

△ The Ciboney, Arawak, and Carib originally came to the Antilles by canoe or raft from northeastern Venezuela via Trinidad. Other peoples settled in the tropical lowlands and fertile river valleys of Colombia, living in large well-built towns. They were farmers and also skillful goldsmiths. In some areas gold was worked 1,000 years before the Spanish Conquest.

Settlement of the Antilles c. 2500 BC to AD 1492

c.2500 BC Ciboney Indians. By 1492 only a few remained in parts of Cuba and Hispaniola.
c.100 BC Arawak Indians. By 1492 they lived in Jamaica, Cuba, the Bahamas, Hispaniola, Puerto Rico, and the Leeward Islands.
c.AD 1200 Carib Indians. By 1492 they lived in the Windward Islands and were pushing into the Leeward Islands. (Also called Caribales or Canibales by early writers, from which came the modern word "cannibal.")
1492 Columbus lands on San Salvador in the Bahamas. Makes Hispaniola (Dominican Republic and Haiti) his base for exploring the Caribbean Islands and the Central and South American coasts.

THE CENTRAL ANDES: CHAVÍN AND PARACAS

The earliest inhabitants of the Andes hunted animals and collected wild plant food, but fishing and farming gradually became more important. Fishing nets were made from cotton twine and floats from hollowed-out gourds. Farmers grew crops such as squash, beans, chili peppers, maize, and potatoes. They kept dogs as pets and for hunting and raised ducks and guinea pigs for food. Herds of llamas and alpacas were bred for their wool and meat, and llamas were also used as pack animals.

Some of the greatest civilizations in the New World developed in this area, like the Moche and Chimu along the coast and the Inca in the highlands. Early peoples often influenced those who came later. When the Inca conquered the Chimu around AD 1470, for example, they borrowed much of their art and way of life.

The Chavín civilization

This civilization takes its name from temple ruins near Chavín de Huantar on the eastern slopes of the Andes. The earliest Chavín sites date from about 1200 BC. Chavín de Huantar itself flourished later, between 850 and 200 BC. The main temple is honeycombed with rooms and passages connected by stairways. It contains a great stone carving of a figure with snarling fangs and snakes instead of hair – probably an important Chavín god. Similar figures are found in the art of people who lived long after the Chavín disappeared.

◁ This carved stone head is one of several fixed into the walls of the temple at Chavín de Huantar. It depicts a supernatural creature, partly human, but with the fangs of a jaguar. Other carvings here show eagles, snakes, caymans, or human beings with the features of these animals. The Chavín art style spread over much of Peru.

Tombs at Paracas

The Paracas peninsula is best known for the large number of tombs which have been found there, dating from between 700 BC to 200 BC. The tombs contained mummified bodies wrapped in layers of cloth to form bundles. The bundles included sets of cotton garments – shirts, mantles, loin-cloths, and turbans – many beautifully embroidered with strange mythical creatures, birds, and animals. The colors of the

▽ The Indians obtained most of their gold by panning in highland streams and rivers. They used "digging sticks" (straight, pointed sticks) to loosen and break up the earth and gravel, which they then washed in shallow wooden trays. In some areas they also dug shafts to mine veins of quartz to extract gold. Silver and copper ores were dug from pits and smelted in clay furnaces.

Copper and bronze were used for weapons and tools, and gold and silver mainly for jewelry and ceremonial objects.

◁ Ceremonial knife *tumi* about AD 1200 from the Lambayeque Valley, northern Peru. The handle may show the Sun God. The elaborate headdress is inlaid with turquoise.

▷ Embroidery from a Paracas mummy bundle. It shows a supernatural being wearing a headband of sheet gold, a kind that has been found in burials.

▽ This pendant of cast tumbaga (a gold/copper alloy) was made in the Tairona area of northeast Colombia about AD 1000. It may represent a super-natural being, part human, part bat, or a priest wearing a bat mask.

wool embroidery remain rich and vivid today, because the dry desert air preserved them.

Metalworking in the Andes

The Andean region was the greatest center of metalworking in America. According to early Spanish writers, the Inca thought of gold as "the sweat of the sun" and silver as "the tears of the moon." The earliest metalwork found – a few scraps of gold foil – dates from about 1500 BC. Later on, gold, silver, copper, and platinum were all worked, and mixed with one another to form alloys. Copper was also alloyed with tin to make bronze.

Smiths worked the metal by hammering it into thin sheets. Shapes were cut to make masks, crowns, ear ornaments, necklaces, and pins. Figurines were also cast in molds.

NAZCA: LINES IN THE DESERT

The Nazca people are named after their sites in the Nazca Valley on the south coast of Peru. They lived in several of the coastal river valleys from about 370 BC to AD 450.

The Nazca may have been related to the people who produced the textiles and other grave goods found at Paracas. The designs used by the Nazca on their textiles and pottery are very similar to those of Paracas. Quantities of both Paracas and Nazca pottery have been found at Ocucje in the Ica Valley.

The ordinary people lived in small villages. Unlike those who lived in the mountains, the coastal people did not have supplies of good stone for building. The Nazca built their houses of wattle and daub or adobe bricks.

The most important Nazca site is the ceremonial center of Cahuachi in the Nazca Valley. The site consists of several terraced pyramids which are in fact natural hills faced with adobe bricks. The largest is 65ft high. Around it were plazas, rooms, and tombs.

▽ The Nazca people made some of the finest pottery in the New World. Painted in rich colours, the pots depict gods and people, animals, birds and plants. This jar, made in the form of a supernatural being, is painted with strange monsters and "trophy heads", probably those of sacrificed captives.

The Nazca Lines

Among the most fascinating of all archaeological puzzles are the so-called "Nazca lines" which cover an area of almost 200 sq. mi northwest of the modern town of Nazca. They were made by removing the dark surface stones to expose the lighter ground below.

The lines vary from 600yd to more than 5mi in length. Some join to form geometric shapes like squares or triangles. Others cross one another or come together at a central point. Not all the lines are straight. Some are in the form of plants and animals – a tree, birds, a spider, a killer whale, a monkey with a long spiraling tail. Since there is no rain to disturb the ground in this desert area, the lines remain just as they were made, over 1,000 years ago.

Gods and stars

Because of their large size, the shapes made by the lines are difficult to recognize on the ground. It was not until the 1920s, when they were viewed from an airplane, that their complete outlines were finally discovered. One of the many puzzles surrounding the lines is how they were plotted so accurately, for the people who made them could only ever have seen them from the ground.

Just as mysterious as *how* the lines were made is *why* they were made. Some writers have suggested that, since they are completely visible only from the air, they may have been offerings to the sky gods. Or, they may have linked sacred places. Others believe that the lines relate to the movements of the planets and were used by farmers as a kind of calendar to predict the weather and so prepare for irrigation of crops. (Rain in the mountains would bring flood water to these dry areas.) Similar markings have been found elsewhere in Peru and in Chile, about 500mi away.

▷ Nazca lines sometimes converge on a center, perhaps a sacred place. A close-up of a "drawing" (far right) shows the scale of the lines.

▽ Some Nazca lines align with the setting sun at certain times of the year, such as the winter solstice (about December 22). These lines may have been laid out by astronomers to help them calculate the movement of the planets.

The Moche people

The site of Moche is on the northern coast of Peru, near the modern city of Trujillo. It was the ceremonial and administrative capital of the Moche people who lived in this area between the 1st and 7th centuries AD.

The Moche were farmers, growing a variety of crops in the river valleys. They built canals and aqueducts to irrigate their fields. Many of these are great feats of engineering and some are still in use today.

We know a great deal about the Moche from pottery found in their graves. Modeled and painted decoration depicts gods, people, houses, plants, and animals. Their everyday activities – hunting, fishing, or weaving – and rituals and ceremonies are shown.

Temples and pyramids

The Moche also built large temples. The most impressive of these are the great twin adobe pyramids at Moche itself. They are known as the Huaca del Sol, Temple of the Sun, and the Huaca de la Luna, Temple of the Moon. (These are names given to them by the Spanish and do not necessarily mean that the temples had anything to do with the worship of the sun or moon.) Both temples consist of terraced platforms and the larger, the Huaca del Sol, has a terraced pyramid on top of it.

The Huaca de la Luna lies at the foot of a hill, Cerro Blanco. It stands about 70ft high and has several rooms and courtyards on top. The Huaca del Sol is probably the largest adobe building in the Americas. In its present form it is 130ft high and about 1,150ft long. Originally it was much larger, but the sides have been damaged both by weather and by treasure hunters. It seems to have been built in a number of stages over several centuries. Its last building stage contained the grave of two people, but it may not have been built as a burial mound originally.

Both temples were probably used for religious ceremonies. Clues to this can be seen on Moche pots. Some show prisoners being sacrificed to fanged beings seated on top of pyramids.

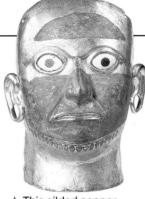

△ This gilded copper mask with shell-inlay eyes was found in a Moche burial. The ear lobes are stretched to take the large, decorative ear plugs worn by men of high rank.

▷ "Stirrup-spout" bottle showing the head of a Moche god. The fangs and snakes curling around the head are reminders of the Chavín fanged god.

▽ Cerro Blanco towers over the Huaca de la Luna at Moche. The temple's main platform, built of adobe bricks, rises about 70ft above the plain. The rooms on top originally had painted wall designs.

Tiahuanaco and Huari empires

Around AD 500-1000 these two empires came to dominate much of the central and southern Andes and parts of the coast. The first is named after the ruins of Tiahuanaco, which lie in modern Bolivia, about 13mi east of Lake Titicaca. The surrounding area, known as the altiplano, is a bleak treeless plateau. It is, however, the largest area of flat farming land in the Andes and people have lived here for thousands of years.

Food plants like potatoes and quinoa (a hardy grain, also called "Andean rice") were probably first grown here. The land provides good grazing for llama and alpaca herds. In addition, the surrounding mountains are rich in gold, silver, copper, and tin.

Tiahuanaco – a great ceremonial center
Many of the great stone buildings at Tiahuanaco seem to have been for ceremonial use. The most impressive are the Akapana, a large terraced pyramid, and the great temple enclosure known as the Kalasasaya.

At the northwest corner of the Kalasasaya is perhaps the best known of the monumental sculptures at Tiahuanaco, the so-called "Gateway of the Sun." The gateway, about 10ft

▷ This sculptured figure stands just inside the Kalasasaya at Tiahuanaco. It is carved from a single block of sandstone, 12ft high. The mask-like face with its staring eyes is typical of the Tiahuanaco art style.

▽ Lake Titicaca on the border of Bolivia and Peru. Situated at nearly 13,200ft above sea level, it is the highest navigable lake in the world. Here local fishermen use a type of ancient boat called a balsa. These boats are made of bundles of reeds bound together. Sails are made of cotton or of woven reed mats. The people of Tiahuanaco used similar boats before the Spanish Conquest.

▽ Part of a wall of the huge sunken courtyard of the Kalasasaya, the largest and most important temple at Tiahuanaco. One of the great gateways of Tiahuanaco is behind.

high, is cut from a single block of stone. At the top is a carved figure wearing a radiating headdress of puma heads. Condor and puma heads are carved on his body and from his belt hangs a row of human faces, perhaps trophy heads from sacrificial victims.

Twin capitals
The second civilization, Huari, was near the modern city of Ayacucho in the southern highlands of Peru. Stone carvings and pottery similar to those at Tiahuanaco are found here, although they tend to be less elaborate.

The two civilizations, although about 400mi apart, were certainly in contact. They shared an art style and perhaps their religion, too. Both expanded their empires around the same time, becoming more powerful and conquering other territories.

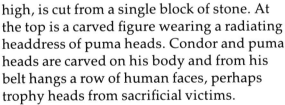

THE INCA EMPIRE

Until about AD 1440 the Inca were only one of several groups of people living in the southern Andes. By defeating their neighbors, they became the most powerful group. Under their great ruler, Pachacuti, the Inca began a campaign of conquest and rapidly expanded their territory, spreading north, south and west. By the eve of the Spanish invasion in 1532 the Inca empire stretched nearly 2,500mi along the western coast of South America from northern Ecuador to central Chile.

Control of the conquered territories

When a new region was conquered, an Inca noble of high rank was chosen to govern it. Local leaders were allowed to keep their posts as long as they remained loyal to the Inca emperor. Their children were taken as hostages to Cuzco, the Inca capital, where they were educated in Inca ways before returning home. Possible troublemakers were moved to other parts of the empire. Loyal colonists were brought in to replace them. This policy of moving people about also meant that new ideas and ways of life were taken to other areas. Farming and irrigation methods, for example, were introduced into regions where they had not existed before.

Governing the empire – the chain of command

Government of the Inca empire was organized like a pyramid, with the emperor, called Sapa Inca, at the top. He was believed to be descended from the sun and was treated as a god. He had absolute power over his subjects.

▷ The Inca called their empire Tahuantinsuyu, meaning "Land of the Four Quarters." The quarters were: Chinchasuya in the north, Cuntisuya in the west, Antisuya in the east and Collasuya in the south. At the center lay Cuzco, the Inca capital. To control their vast empire, the Inca built a great network of roads, often over difficult mountain land.

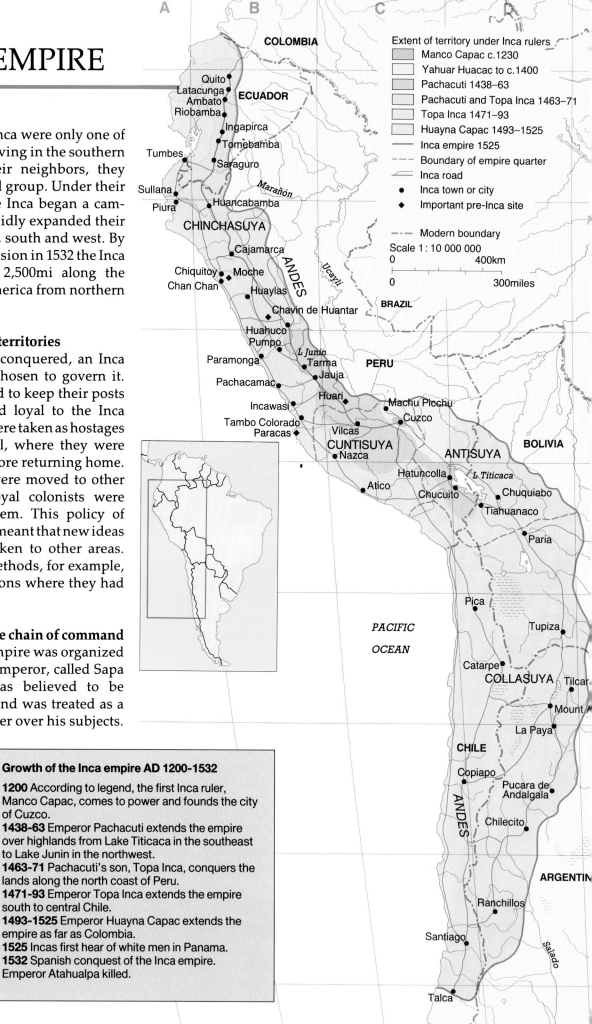

Growth of the Inca empire AD 1200-1532

1200 According to legend, the first Inca ruler, Manco Capac, comes to power and founds the city of Cuzco.

1438-63 Emperor Pachacuti extends the empire over highlands from Lake Titicaca in the southeast to Lake Junin in the northwest.

1463-71 Pachacuti's son, Topa Inca, conquers the lands along the north coast of Peru.

1471-93 Emperor Topa Inca extends the empire south to central Chile.

1493-1525 Emperor Huayna Capac extends the empire as far as Colombia.

1525 Incas first hear of white men in Panama.

1532 Spanish conquest of the Inca empire. Emperor Atahualpa killed.

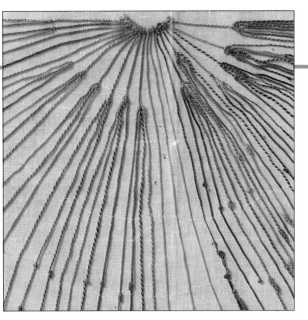

When he died his body was preserved in his palace where servants continued to wait on him. At great festivals the mummies of long-dead Sapa Incas were carried in ceremonial procession through the streets of Cuzco.

Below the Sapa Inca were the governors of the four quarters of the empire and below them the governors of the provinces into which each quarter was divided. Underneath the provincial governors were local rulers and leaders. At the bottom were the ordinary people or commoners. Their lives were strictly controlled. They were not allowed to travel without official permission. Luxury goods, such as silver or gold objects, were reserved for the nobility.

Farming and work service

Most commoners were farmers. Each family in a community was given land according to its needs. Remaining fields were divided between the gods and the emperor. Farmers had to work these fields as well as their own.

The harvests from the religious and imperial fields were gathered into separate storehouses. Food from the religious storehouse fed the priests and provided offerings to the gods. Produce from the emperor's storehouse supported the nobles, the army, state officials and craftsmen, as well as those who were too old or sick to provide for themselves.

Each commoner had to do some work service for the government every year. Known as the mit'a, it could involve serving in the army, laboring in mines and quarries, or building and maintaining roads and bridges.

▽ Inca cities had very efficient drainage and water-supply systems. A series of finely carved stone channels and basins carried water down through the mountain city of Machu Picchu. Shown here is one such channel.

◁ Remains of stonebuilt shrines at Tambomachay, just east of Cuzco, show the great skill of Inca stonemasons. The terraces and walls contain and channel a sacred spring (religious sites were built around springs from earliest times). The four niches at the top may represent the caves from which, according to myth, the original Inca people emerged.

Cuzco – the great Inca capital

Cuzco was founded about AD 1200. In the 15th century the emperor Pachacuti changed it from a town of wood and thatch to a great stone city which enormously impressed the Spanish invaders. Present-day Cuzco is built on Inca remains. It is probably the oldest continuously occupied city in South America.

Cuzco was the hub of the Inca empire. The "four quarters" into which the empire was divided radiated from Cuzco's central plaza, the Huacacapata. The emperor's palace was the seat of government from which the empire was ruled. The Temple of the Sun was the Inca's most sacred shrine. Statues of the gods and other sacred objects were stored there. The walls were hung with elaborate tapestries and plated with gold and silver. Only priests and very important officials entered the temple. Most ceremonies were performed out of doors in the Huacacapata.

△ Part of the Temple of the Sun beneath the church of Santo Domingo in Cuzco. The temple was the ceremonial heart of the Inca capital and empire.

▽ Walls of Sacsahuaman, a great fortress built above Cuzco to hold up to 10,000 people. Fierce battles were fought here in the 1530s in the Spanish Conquest.

Machu Picchu · Cuzco

Machu Picchu

The ruins of the Inca city of Machu Picchu occupy one of the world's most spectacular ancient sites. The city, about 43mi northwest of Cuzco, is built on a rocky ridge surrounded by high mountains. On either side the land slopes away in manmade terraces before dropping 2,000ft to the valley of the Urubamba river below. The city is visible on one side only – from a mountain road on the south. From the river valley it is completely invisible.

Mountain farmers

The ruins consist of nearly 300 buildings of stone arranged on either side of an oblong plaza. Farming families lived in one-roomed houses grouped around a central courtyard. Inside, the houses would have been dark and smoky, but people would mostly have been out in the courtyard or in the fields.

A stone aqueduct brought a supply of fresh water from the mountain streams. A system of channels and basins carried the water through the city and down to the farming terraces on the lower slopes.

Excellent builders in stone

The Inca were highly skilled architects, engineers and stonemasons. Machu Picchu is the great example of their achievement in building in difficult mountainous areas.

Stonemasons' tools consisted of stone and bronze chisels, hammers, and crowbars. Blocks of stone were worked into shape with hammers. The blocks were often rounded at the edges or polished so that they caught the light and made patterns. The masons cut the blocks to fit so well that no mortar was needed. The joints are usually so tight that it is impossible to slip a knife blade between them. Many Inca walls stand today, in spite of the earthquakes that shake the Andes.

◁ This view of Machu Picchu shows its dramatic mountain setting and the skillful way in which the builders used the natural contours of the site. Just visible are characteristic Inca doorways and niches. These are not perfectly rectangular in shape but narrower at the top than at the bottom.

CONTROLLING THE INCA EMPIRE

The Inca needed roads to transport goods, move troops, and send messages. Without good roads it would have been impossible for them to govern their far-flung empire.

There were no wheeled vehicles in Peru (or anywhere else in pre-Conquest America). Goods were carried on people's backs or on llamas. Although roads were built in a straight line wherever possible, they could zigzag up steep slopes or be replaced by steps.

Travelers on the road

Government permission was needed by those who wished to use roads. Most people walked, but those of high rank were carried in litters. A 16th-century Spanish chronicler, Cieza de Leon, noted the splendor of emperors' travel:

> When the Incas visited the provinces of their empire in time of peace, they traveled in great majesty, seated in rich litters fitted with loose poles of excellent wood... enriched with gold and silver work... there were two high arches set with precious stones, and long mantles fell round all sides of the litter so as to cover it...

As well as officials, armies, and llama pack-trains on the roads, there were government messengers who provided a 24-hour service. Relay stations, about 1mi apart, housed a pair of runners. They received messages brought by runners from the previous station and carried them on to the next. In this way messages could be carried about 150mi per day.

▷ Inca roads were often triumphs of engineering, especially in mountain areas. Sometimes their surface was paved. They were carried over rivers on bridges, over marshland on causeways and occasionally through hills in tunnels. Here an important person is being carried in a litter on the shoulders of four bearers.

Deep ravines were crossed by suspension bridges, made of cables of twisted plant fibre. These bridges could be anything up to 200ft length! Although they swayed alarmingly in the wind, they seem to have been quite safe for foot-travelers and pack animals. Some were in use until the 19th century.

▽ Tambo Colorado on the south coast of Peru. Tambos, or rest-houses, were built along the roads. They were about a day's journey apart and were for the use of official travelers. They contained supplies of equipment, clothing, and food. Local communities were responsible for the upkeep of the tambos in their areas.

ANDEAN TEXTILES

People have been making cloth in Peru for at least 6,000 years. The earliest textiles were made from cotton, which grows wild in this region. People began to plant and grow cotton from about 3500 BC. Later the glossy wool of the domesticated llama and alpaca was used as well as the finer, silkier fleece of the wild vicuña.

Spinning, dyeing, and weaving

Early textiles were often rather coarse. Later people learned to spin fine yarn using delicate wooden spindles. Unless a weaver decided to use the natural colors of the yarn, dyeing was usually the next step. Most dyes came from plants. Leaves, flowers, and berries were collected and boiled up to produce a range of brilliant dyes. Archaeologists studying the Paracas embroideries have found nearly 200 different colors in the designs.

The weaver sat in front of a narrow loom hung from a rafter or a peg in the wall, or from the branch of a tree if she preferred to work out of doors. The same sort of loom is still used in Peru today. The cloth woven could only be as wide as the span of the weaver's arms as she passed the yarn from side to side. If a larger cloth were needed – for a cloak perhaps – several lengths of cloth had to be stitched together.

Peruvian costume

Most people wore a loose sleeveless tunic made from two pieces of cloth with openings for the head and arms. Ponchos were made in the same way but with sides left open. Inca tunics were sometimes made from one long piece of cloth with a slit in the center for the wearer's head. Both men and women wore cloaks fastened with a large pin. Clothing of important people was richly embroidered or decorated with feathers or with metal or shell pendants.

Men wore caps or turbans, sometimes tied under the chin. Women often went bareheaded or pulled their cloaks over their heads. Inca men and women wore headbands and women also covered their heads with a folded cloth. The Inca emperor wore a special headband hung with red tassels encased in gold tubes.

Women's work

Women did most of the spinning and weaving. A married woman was responsible for making

▽ This strange creature, half cat, half bird, is embroidered on cloth from a Paracas mummy bundle. The dry desert conditions at Paracas preserved it for over 2,000 years.

▷ (left) A man's cap of woven wool shaped with a point at each corner. Such caps are typical of Huari-Tiahuanaco ceremonial costume. They are shown in pottery and carving.

▷ (right) Feathers from tropical forests were attached to a backing of woven cotton to make ceremonial garments like this neckpiece (north coast of Peru, c. AD 1200-1470).

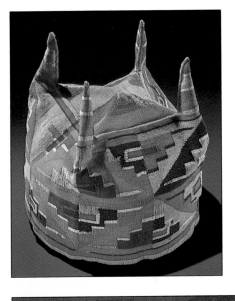

all her family's clothing and took great pride in doing so. This work was considered so important that women often had their spinning and weaving tools buried with them.

Under the Incas, the wife of a commoner had to provide one woven garment per year as part of her family's tax payment to the emperor. The daughters of commoners were sometimes chosen by agents of the emperor to be educated at special schools or convents. Here they were taught to spin and weave cotton and wool to a high standard in preparation for their future lives as priestesses or as wives of nobles. Even women of the royal family learned to spin and weave. When the emperor's wife or daughter traveled around the country, she was accompanied by servants carrying her tools and yarn so that her work continued wherever she went.

Beautiful textiles and clothing were very important to the ancient Peruvians. They were used as religious offerings and as gifts on special occasions. At the ceremony held to name an Inca baby, for example, relatives gave the baby presents of wool and fine clothing. When people died, large quantities of clothing and textiles were buried with them.

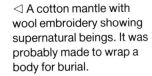

◁ A cotton mantle with wool embroidery showing supernatural beings. It was probably made to wrap a body for burial.

▽ The loom most commonly used in ancient Peru. The weaver's costume and hat is typical of the Cuzco region.

SURVIVALS OF EVERYDAY LIFE AND RITUALS

In Latin America many aspects of the ancient way of life continue to survive. For example, buldings are still constructed using traditional materials like stone, cane, and adobe. In the highlands of Peru houses are still thatched with the same grass as they were in Inca times.

Many of the foodstuffs that people in Latin America eat today are direct descendants of those grown thousands of years ago. Although wheat and barley are grown nowadays, maize remains the most important crop and of course has spread to other parts of the world. There are a number of Indian foods that have been brought to Europe over the centuries and have become familiar items in our own diet. As well as maize and its relation, sweet corn, these foods include potatoes, tomatoes, pineapples, avocados, several kinds of beans and peppers, peanuts, and chocolate.

▷ Inca farmers harvested potatoes and made holes for planting seed using a footplow. This was like a curved digging stick with a footrest near the pointed end. Here, present-day farmers are seen using footplows to break up the ground on a farming terrace in Peru. These tools have been shown to suit shallow soil better than modern mechanical plows.

◁ During the Inca's rule of their empire, markets were held in each district where local people could exchange their surplus produce and goods like fruit, vegetables, or pottery. Peruvian villagers today still hold markets on ancient Inca sites. The one shown here takes place once a week at Chinchero, a town near Cuzco. The goods on display are much the same as those bartered in Inca times. Women still carry their produce or purchases in large cloths on their backs, just as their ancestors did.

▷ The first Indians seen by Columbus were "*all naked and painted white, red, black*." Amazon Indians still paint their bodies, on special occasions. Here two Yanomamo women decorate each other for a feast using paint made from plants.

▽ The Tarahumara Indians of northern Mexico perform the Dance of the Pharisees during Holy Week (the week before Easter). For this they paint their bodies and wear chicken or turkey feather crowns. They dance with a straw effigy of Judas, who betrayed Jesus.

The Spanish introduced several new domestic animals into the Americas. In the Andes, for example, llamas have been largely replaced by sheep for meat and wool and by donkeys as pack animals. Alpacas are still kept for their wool, for weaving continues both for the Indians' own use and for the tourist trade. Many weavers, however, find it easier to buy ready-spun yarn or to use chemical dyes which produce brighter colors than plant dyes.

Rituals and sacred places

Indian religion still flourishes, closely intertwined with the official Latin American religion, Catholicism. Jesus Christ is often identified with the old sun god and the Virgin Mary with the moon goddess (by the Maya) or with the earth goddess (in the Andes). On feast days people carry statues of the Christian saints

△ Modern Indian clothing is a mixture of Indian and Spanish colonial styles. These town officers in the Mexican state of Chiapas wear Indian ponchos over European-style shirts and trousers.

through the streets just as they carried statues of the gods in pre-Conquest times.

Like their ancestors, the Indians also believe in the supernatural power of certain places or objects. Caves, rocks, trees, and streams are often seen as holy places and offerings are made to the gods who inhabit them.

In the Andes cloth is still regarded as a precious offering. In some areas sacred bundles of cloth are unwrapped and displayed at annual ceremonies held to bless crops and livestock. At the end of the ceremony the bundle is wrapped up and hidden away until the following year.

GLOSSARY

agave A type of cactus. It was used as a food and to make an alcoholic drink.

cactus A prickly desert plant, characterized by large, tough stems, brightly colored flowers and leaves reduced to spines or scales.

chinampa A small plot of land reclaimed from the mud of lakes in Central Mexico. The plots were used for growing crops.

Conquistadores A Spanish word for "conquerers." It is usually applied to the Spanish conquerers of Mexico and Peru in the 16th century.

copal A hard aromatic yellow, orange or red resin from various tropical trees. It was used in varnishes as well as for incense.

Eskimo (Inuit) The inhabitants of the Arctic coasts and islands. There are two main groups – the Yupik who inhabit eastern Siberia and southern and central Alaska and the Inuit who stretch from northern Alaska to Greenland. In Canada "Inuit" (meaning "people") has come to replace "Eskimo," the name given by Indians and later adopted by Europeans.

gorget A breast ornament of stone, shell or metal with holes for wearing on a cord around the neck.

hunters and gatherers People who live by hunting animals and gathering wild plants for food.

Ice Age A period of cold climate when much of the Earth's surface was covered with ice. There were in fact several Ice Ages. The last one began about 70,000 years ago and ended only about 10,000 years ago.

Iroquois A term usually restricted to the Indian groups who allied to form the League of the Iroquois in the 16th century – the Seneca, Cayuga, Onondaga, Oneida, Mohawk and Tuscarora.

Iroquoian A term referring to all Indian groups speaking Iroquoian languages.

litter A vehicle in the form of a chair or couch carried on poles on men's shoulders.

mesquite A thorny shrub bearing edible beanlike pods. It grows in Mexico and the southwestern United States.

Mestizo The name given in Latin America to a person of mixed Indian and European descent.

mica A mineral-bearing rock which can be split into thin transparent sheets.

native A local inhabitant of a country. In America the term refers to the Indians. Today many Indians prefer to be called Native Americans.

nomadic The term used to describe those who wander from place to place, usually in search of food.

Norse The people of ancient Scandinavia, especially Norway.

prehistoric The term used to describe the period in history before the appearance of written records. In American Indian history this is usually taken to mean before 1492 (the year Columbus arrived).

quetzal bird A Central American bird of the pheasant family, prized for its brightly colored feathers.

sarcophagus A stone coffin, often decorated with sculpture or carving.

semidesert Land which is very dry but where it is still possible for some plants to grow for part of the year at least.

stirrup-spout A hollow handle and spout in the shape of a stirrup (a horserider's footrest). A typical feature of Moche pottery.

supernatural Beyond the ordinary forces of nature, to do with gods and other mysterious beings.

travois A wheelless vehicle used by the Plains Indians of North America to carry their belongings. It consisted of a V-shaped framework of poles fastened to an animal's back and dragged along the ground behind it. They were pulled by dogs and (after about 1700) by horses.

FURTHER READING

Reference books
Penny Bateman, *Aztecs and Incas* (Franklin Watts) 1988
Judith Crosher, *The Aztecs* (Silver Burdett Press) 1977
Derek Fordham, *Eskimos* (Silver Burdett Press) 1979
Virginia Luling, *Indians of the North American Plains* (Silver Burdett Press) 1978
Geoffrey Turner, *Indians of North America* (Sterling) 1980
Myths and legends
E.E. Clark, *Indian Legends of the Pacific Northwest* (University of California) 1958
Douglas Gifford, *Warriors, Gods and Spirits from Central and South American Mythology* (Schocken Books) 1983
Z. Nungak and E. Arima, *Eskimo Stories/Unikkaatuat* (Ottawa) 1969
Marion Wood, *Spirits, Heroes and Hunters from North American Indian Mythology* (Schocken Books) 1982

Reference books for adults
G. Bankes, *Peru before Pizarro* (Phaidon) 1977
Jules B. Billard(ed.), *The World of the American Indian* (National Geographic Society) 1974
G.H.S. Bushnell, *Peru* (Thames and Hudson) 1957
M.D.Coe, *Mexico* (Thames and Hudson) 1986
Michael Coe, Dean Snow and Elizabeth Benson, *Atlas of Ancient America* (Facts On File) 1986
J.D. Jennings, *Prehistory of North America* (Mayfield) 1974
Dean Snow, *The American Indians: Their Archaeology and Prehistory* (Thames and Hudson) 1976
G.R. Willey, *An Introduction to American Archaeology. Vol.I North and Middle America. Vol.II South America* (Prentice-Hall) 1969

GAZETTEER

The gazetteer lists places and features, such as islands or mountains found on the maps. Each has a separate entry including a page and grid reference number. For example:

Adena 25 D3

All features are shown in italic type. For example:

Aconcagua, mt. 9 D2

A letter after the feature describes the kind of feature:

d. district; *i.* island;
isls. islands; *mt.* mountain;
mts. mountains

Abaj Takalik 54 C1, 57 E5, 63 B2
Acolhuacan, d. 70 B3
Aconcagua, mt. 9 D2
Adena 25 D3
Adena Park 25 D3
Alaska Range, mts. 9 A7
Aleutian Islands 20 A2
Alibates 18 C2
Altar de Sacrificios 54 C2
Amazonia, d. 13 D3
Ambato 82 B8
Ameca 67 A3
Ammassalik 21 H3
Anaktuvuk Pass 20 B3
Ancohuma, mt. 9 D3
Andes, mts. 9 D3, 82 B7
Andrews 18 E3
Angel 27 C3
Antilles, d. 13 D4
Antilles, Greater, isls. 75 B3
Antilles, Lesser, isls. 9 E4, 75 D3
Antisuya, d. 82 D6
Antonio Plaza 57 C2
Apatzingan 67 A2
Appalachian Mountains 9 D5, 25 D3, 27 D3
Arctic, d. 13 C7
Armadillo 54 B3
Armstrong 18 D3
Arroyo Sonso 57 C2
Arzberger 32 D2
Asunción 9 E2
Asunción Mita 63 C2
Atazta 67 C2
Atico 82 C5
Atlan, d. 70 C4
Atotonilco, d. 70 B4
Atotonilco, d. 70 B3
Axocopan, d. 70 B4
Aztalan 27 C4

Baffin Island 9 D7, 13 D7, 21 G3
Bahamas, isls. 13 D5
Balancán 57 E6
Barriles 75 B2
Bat Cave 18 C2
Baum 27 D3
Becan 63 C4
Bedford 25 B3
Bell 21 E3
Belmopan 9 D4

Beluga Point 20 B3
Bent 18 F3
Betanci 75 B2
Big Hidatsa 32 C3
Bighorn Medicine Wheel 32 B2
Big Sycamore 36 B1
Birch 18 E3
Birnirk 20 B4
Blackduck 27 B5
Bloody Falls 21 D3
Bogotá 9 D4
Bonampak 63 B3
Boone 25 B4
Borax Cave 18 A2
Boucher 25 F4
Bowmans Brook 27 F4
Brand 18 D2
Brasília 9 E3
Brazilian Highlands 9 E3
Brohm 18 E3
Brooks River 20 B2
Bryce Canyon 36 C2
Buchanan 21 E3
Buenos Aires 9 E2
Buritaca 75 C2
Bynum 25 C2

Cahokia 27 B3
Cajamarca 82 B7
Calakmul 63 C4
Calima, d. 75 B1
Calixtlahuaca 67 B2
Campbell Mound 25 D4
Canapote 75 B2
Capacha 54 A2
Caracas 9 D4
Cascade Range, mts. 9 B6, 36 A3
Catarpe 82 D4
Cato 25 C3
Cayenne 9 E4
Cempoala 67 B2, 70 C3
Cerro de la Bomba 54 B2
Chalcatzinco 54 B2, 57 D6
Chalchihuites 67 A3
Chalchuapa 54 D1, 57 E5
Chalco, d. 70 B3
Chalk Hollow 18 C2
Chance 27 F4
Chan Chan 82 B7
Chapultepec 67 B2
Chavín de Huantar 82 B7
Chiapa de Corzo 54 C2
Chichén Itzá 63 C5, 67 D3
Chichimeca Desert 67 A3
Chilecito 82 D3
Chinchasuya, d. 82 B7
Chiquihuitillo 67 A3
Chiquitoy 82 B7
Chirikof Island 20 B2
Choris 20 B3
Chucalissa 27 C3
Chucuito 82 D5
Chugachik Island 20 B3
Chupicuaro 54 A3
Chuquiabo 82 D5
Ciénaga de Oro 75 B2
Cihuatlan, d. 70 A2
Circum Caribbean, d. 13 D4
Claiborne 18 E2
Clasons Point 27 F4
Clay Mound 27 D3
Clemsons Island 27 E4
Coast Mountains 9 B6, 48 C2
Coast Range, mts. 48 D1
Cobá 63 D5

Coixtlahuacan, d. 70 C2
Cojumatlan 67 A3
Collasuya, d. 82 D4
Comalcalco 63 A4
Comitán 54 C2
Copán 54 D1, 63 C2
Copiapo 82 C3
Cow Point 18 G3
Coxcatlan Cave 54 B2
Coyolapan, d. 70 C2
Crab Orchard 25 C3
Craig Harbour 21 F4
Crespo 75 B2
Criel Mound 25 D3
Crow Creek 32 D2
Crus del Milagro 57 A2
Crystall II 21 G3
Cuahuacan, d. 70 B3
Cuauhnahuac, d. 70 B3
Cuauhtitlan, d. 70 B3
Cuauhtochco, d. 70 C3
Cuba, i. 13 D5
Cuetlaxtlan, d. 70 C3
Cueva Humida 54 B3
Culhuacan 67 B2
Cuntisuya, d. 82 C6
Cuzco 13 D3, 82 C6

Dalles, The 18 A3
Danger Cave 18 B3, 36 C3
Davis 27 B2
Death Valley 36 B2
de Blicquy 21 E4
Deer Canyons 36 B1
Deltatefrasserne 21 H5
Diablo 54 B3
Diana Bay 21 F3
Dickson 27 D4
Dirty Shame Rockshelter 36 B3
Dismal Lake 21 D3
Dodemansbugten 21 I4
Dodge Island 48 B2
Doerschuk 18 F2
Dorset, Cape 21 F3
Double Adobe 18 C2
Double Ditch 32 C3
Double House Village 36 B4
Dripping Springs 36 B1
Drunken Point 18 E3
Dundas Island 21 E4
Dust Devil 18 B2
Dyer 18 E3
Dzibilchaltún 54 D3, 63 C5

Eastern Highlands, d. 13 E3
Eastern Prairie 32 D3
Eastern Subarctic, d. 13 D6
Eastern Woodlands, d. 13 C6, 32 E3
Edzná 63 B4
El Baúl 63 B2
El Cafetal 75 B2
El Chayal 54 C1
El Indio 75 B2
Elk Island 18 D4
Ellis Landing 36 A2
El Mesón 56 A4
El Mirador 63 C3
El Opeño 54 A3
El Teul 67 A3
El Viejón 57 D6
Emerald Mound 27 B2
Emeryville Shellmound 36 A2
Engigstciak 20 C3
Esilao 48 D1

Estero Rabón 57 B2
Etowah 27 D2
Eva 18 E2

Fanning 32 D1
Fisher 27 D4
Five Mile Rapids 36 A4, 48 D1
Florence 27 C2
Fort Ancient 25 D3
Fort Walton 27 C2

Galapagos Islands 9 C3
Gargamelle Cove 21 G2
Garoga 27 F4
Gatecliff Shelter 36 B2
Georgetown 9 E4
Glacier Bay 48 A3
Gods Lake 18 D4
Goodall 25 C4
Graham Cave 18 D2
Gran Chaco, d. 13 D2
Grand Rapids 18 D4
Grand Village 27 B2
Grave Creek Mound 25 D3
Great Basin 9 C6, 13 C6, 36 B3
Great Plains 9 C6
Greenland, i. 13 E7, 21 H4
Guatavita 75 C1
Guatemala City 9 C4
Guayabo de Turrialba 75 B2
Guiana Highlands 9 D4
Guida Farm 27 F4
Gulf Hazard 21 F2

Hardaway 18 E2
Hathaway 18 G3
Hatuncolla 82 D5
Havana 9 D5
Havana 25 C4
Hickson Petroglyph 36 B2
High Plains 32 C2
Hispaniola, i. 13 D4, 75 C3
Hiwassee Island 27 D3
Hogup Cave 18 B3, 36 C3
Hoko River 48 D1
Hooper Bay 20 B3
Hopewell 25 D3
Horn, Cape 9 D1
Howard Lake 25 B4
Huahuco 82 B7
Huancabamba 82 B7
Huari 82 C6
Huaxtepec, d. 70 B3
Huaylas 82 B7
Huber 27 D4
Huehuetenango 54 C2
Hueipochtlan, d. 70 B4
Huff 32 C3
Hungary Hall 18 D3

Iceland, i. 13 F7, 21 I3
Igloolik 21 F3
Illummersuit 21 G4
Illutalik 21 H3
Imaha 21 F3
Incawasi 82 B6
Indian Knoll 18 E2
Ingapirca 82 B8
Inglefield Land 21 G4
Inussuk 21 G4
Inverhuron 18 E3
Ipiutak 20 B3
Islona de Chantuto 54 C2
Itinnera 21 G3
Itztepetl 67 A3

Ixtlan 67 A3
Iyatayet 20 B3
Izamal 63 C5, 67 D3
Izapa 54 C1, 57 E5, 63 A2

Jackson 21 D4
Jaina 63 B5
Jaketown 18 D2, 25 B2
Jauja 82 B6
Joss 21 D4
Juxtlahuaca 54 B2, 57 D6

Kabah 63 C5
Kaminaljuyu 63 B2
Kangeq 21 G3
Kap Holbaek 21 I5
Karlo Site 36 A3
Kathio 27 B5
Kelso 27 E4
Kemp 27 D3
Key Marco 27 D1
Kings Beach 36 A2
Kings Mounds 27 C3
Knapp Mounds 27 B3
Knight 25 B3
Kolnaes Umiak 21 I5
Kolomoki 27 D2
Koster 18 D2
Kukak 20 B2
Kurigitavik 20 B3
Kuujjua River 21 D4

Labná 63 C5
Labrador 9 D6, 13 D6
Lady Franklin Point 21 D3
Laguna de los Cerros 54 B2, 57 A3
La Honradez 63 C3
La India 75 B3
La Jolla 18 B2
Lake Jackson 27 D2
Lake Mohave 18 B2
Lamar 27 D2
Lamoka Lake 18 F3
L'Anse aux Meadows 13 E6
La Paya 82 D3
La Paz 9 D3
La Perra 54 B3
La Quemada 67 A3
Las Bocas 57 D6
Las Flores 67 B3
Las Limas 57 A1
Las Victorias 54 D1
Latacunga 82 B8
La Venta 57 C3
Leary 32 D2
Leeward Islands 75 D3
Le Montaña 75 B2
Leó 67 A3
Lima 9 D3, 13 D3
Little Harbor Site 18 B2
Little Sycamore 36 B1
Logan Creek 18 D3
Lonesome Creek 21 G5
Los Idolos 57 B2
Los Mangos 57 A3
Los Remedios 67 B2
Los Soldados 57 C3
Los Tapiales 54 C2
Lovelock Cave 36 B3
Lower Hidatsa 32 C3
Lubaantun 63 C3

McConnell 18, E3
Machaquilá 63 C3
Machu Picchu 82 C6

INDEX